# A TASTE of the WORLD

# A TASTE of the WORLD

## Celebrating Global Flavors

Rowena Scherer

THE
collective
BOOK STUDIO

Acknowledgments

Thanks to Adelaide Mueller
for her contribution to the recipes.

Nick Shaw and Ashley Skatoff
for their photography contributions.

Library of Congress Cataloging-in-Publication Data available.
ISBN: 978-1-68555-172-8
Ebook ISBN: 978-1-68555-855-0
Library of Congress Control Number: 2023906127

Manufactured in China.
Design by Liliana Guia.
Illustrations by Albert Pew.
Photographs by Nick Shaw & Ashley Skatoff.
10 9 8 7 6 5 4 3 2 1

The Collective Book Studio®
Oakland, California
www.thecollectivebook.studio

# FOOD IS A LENS FOR CULTURE.

—Dana Goodyear

# Hello, Explorers!

Here's a little story about how eat2explore came to be! I created eat2explore as an experiential way to teach my children world cultures and cooking skills. The inspiration came during a vacation cooking class, when I discovered that although my kids loved to travel and taste different cuisines, they couldn't even chop an onion!

You see, growing up in Malaysia, some of my fondest memories were in the kitchen cooking with my family. It was during those moments that I developed my palate and sustainable consumption habits, as well as confidence and independence. But after years working on Wall Street and living in fascinating places around the world, life became too busy for family meals. I realized I needed to start creating lasting memories at home, while also instilling the important life skills I learned as a child.

So, I took the things I treasured the most—family, food, travel, and education—and created an opportunity for all children to discover cuisines from around the world. I went to the French Culinary Institute, and later I began to source hard-to-find nonperishable ingredients to highlight locally cherished foods from around the world. I started eat2explore with a team of trusted educators and created an explorer box filled with authentic recipes, activities, and collectibles that offer a one-of-a-kind, award-winning cultural education through food exploration.

After its success, it was logical to compile the recipes from the boxes into a book. Here, we've chosen the most popular recipes from across the globe, organized by continent and country. We hope you like this sampling of world cuisines and that it inspires you to start cooking.

 Happy cooking!

# How to Use This Book

As you cook your way through this book, you'll notice a few unique elements.

## Stars
Each recipe shows 1, 2, or 3 stars to indicate the skill level needed to do each step. For each recipe, you'll find a task appropriate for whatever age child is cooking with you.

★ = youngest chefs (ages 3 to 8)
★★ = older chefs (ages 9 to 14)
★★★ = oldest chefs (ages 15 and up)

## Special Diets
Each recipe indicates whether it is
- **Dairy-Free**
- **Nut-Free**
- **Gluten-Free**

Also, in many cases, the ingredients list will offer alternative ingredients that, if chosen, will make the recipe easily gluten-free.

## Vegetarian or Vegan Options
For many of the recipes, we've included an option to make the recipe vegetarian. If you choose to make your dish vegetarian, simply use the ingredients under that heading instead of the meat called for in the recipe. You will use all the other ingredients in the list. Any vegetarian alterations to the recipe will be clearly called out in the instructions.

Many of the vegetarian options will also make the dish vegan. Look for the Allergens icon ⊘, use the Vegetarian Option ingredients, and you're good to go.

## Spice and Sauce Mixes

Each recipes uses one or more mixes that include a variety of herbs, spices, and other ingredients that are meant to be mixed together and then added to the recipe where instructed. These mixes are also available to purchase online at eat2explore, which will make cooking the recipes even easier! These spices and herbs are often the key flavor component that makes the recipes unique to their respective countries. Use the QR code below to access our website where you can order the mixes.

## Basic Pantry Items

The following ingredients are those that many people already have in their pantries or refrigerators. When you are making out your shopping list, be sure to check and see whether you already have some of the ingredients you need. This will save you from double buying an ingredient you might not use very much.

- **All-purpose flour or gluten-free flour**
- **Baking powder**
- **Butter**
- **Cornstarch**
- **Honey**
- **Milk**
- **Oil (olive or other vegetable oil)**
- **Pepper**
- **Salt**
- **Sugar**

## Glossary

There are many unusual foods and cooking terms used in the book, so we've placed a glossary in the back (page 224) with short definitions.

# Tips for Successful Cooking

If you follow these basic tips before you start cooking, you'll find that it's easier to make each recipe and you'll be less likely to forget an ingredient or find yourself scrambling for the right equipment while you are in the middle of cooking.

**Safety First!**
Be sure to keep smaller children away from sharp knives and hot stove tops and ovens. There are plenty of safe tasks for younger children in each recipe that will help them build their skills.

**Wash your hands.**
Don't forget to use soap.

**Be ready to cook.**
Tie back long hair; roll up sleeves. Cooking can be messy—use an apron and have kitchen towels or paper towels ready to clean up spills.

**Read the recipe all the way through before you begin.**
It will get you familiar with the ingredients and the necessary steps you'll need to complete the recipe.

**Assemble the ingredients on the countertop before you start cooking.**
Professional chefs do this all the time and they call it "mise en place," which is just French for "everything in its place." By having all your ingredients ready to go, you won't forget to add an important ingredient and you won't need to chase one down at the last second.

**Assemble any equipment you need before you start cooking.**
The same goes for the tools you use to cook. Think about what you might need to use, whether it's a skillet, spoons, a certain knife, a colander, or even paper towels.

# Explore Asia

The continent of Asia is the largest and most populous in the world. According to the United Nations, there are 48 countries in Asia, including China, which has the largest population of any other country. Russia is the world's largest country in size and borders both China and Europe.

This section features recipes from five Asian countries:

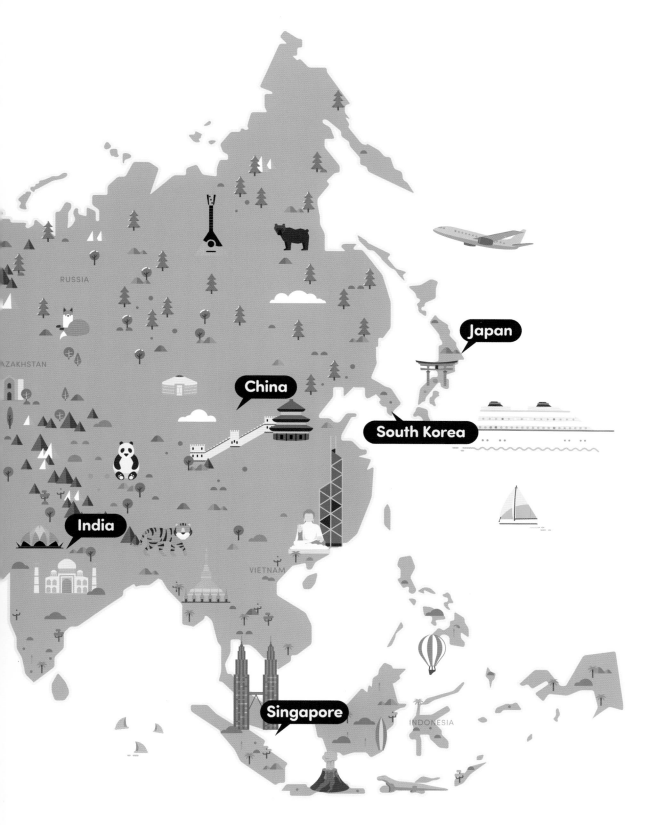

# Japan

Japan is a group of nearly 7,000 islands (which is called an archipelago), and only around 400 or so are inhabited. Japan has access to the Pacific Ocean and the Sea of Japan, so fish are naturally a staple diet of the Japanese people. According to the Food and Agriculture Organization of the United Nations, each person in Japan eats more than 123 pounds of fish per year—that's more than 4 pounds of fish per week!

頂きます
Itadakimasu!
(EE-tah-dah-kee-MAHSS)
*"Thanks for the food!" in Japanese*

**YOU'LL COOK:**

**Broiled Salmon or Chicken with Spinach, and Rice (Teriyaki)**

**Breaded and Fried Pork or Chicken, Cabbage, and Potato Salad (Katsuretsu)**

**Japanese Cabbage Pancakes with Mayo and Bonito Flakes (Okonomiyaki)**

# Broiled Salmon or Chicken with Spinach and Rice
## Teriyaki

Pronounced "teh-ree-YAH-kee," the name is a combination of two words: "teri" or "tare," which refers to the shine from the sugar glaze, and "yaki," which indicates the cooking method of grilling or broiling.

 **SERVES**
4

 **ALLERGENS**
Dairy-Free, Nut-Free

 **TOTAL PREP & COOK TIME**
50 minutes + 2 hours or overnight to marinate

### What You'll Need

4 garlic cloves

3 scallions

1 tablespoon olive oil, plus more to grease the baking sheet

4 (6-oz) salmon fillets or 1½ pounds boneless chicken breasts or thighs

1½ cups short-grain rice

Salt

10 ounces fresh spinach

1 tablespoon sesame oil

Pepper

### NORI SESAME

1 tablespoon nori seaweed flakes

1 tablespoon sesame seeds

### YUMMY TERIYAKI SAUCE

¼ cup soy sauce

¼ cup mirin

2 tablespoons sake or cooking sake (optional)

1 tablespoon sugar

2 teaspoons ground ginger

1 teaspoon sesame oil

### 1. Prep the ingredients ★★

- **Garlic**—Peel and mince or crush with a garlic press.
- **Scallions**—Trim the ends and thinly slice. Use half in step 2 and half in step 6.
- **Nori Sesame**—Combine the nori and sesame seeds in a small bowl.

### 2. Marinate the salmon or chicken (at least 2 hours ahead or overnight) ★

- **Yummy Teriyaki Sauce**—Combine all the ingredients in a large bowl and mix well.
- Add the minced garlic, half of the scallions, and 1 tablespoon of olive oil and mix well.
- Add the salmon or chicken and mix well. Cover and marinate in the refrigerator for at least 2 hours or overnight.

### 3. Cook the rice ★★

- Rinse the rice in a colander to remove excess starch.
- In a small pot, combine the rice, a pinch of salt, and 2¼ cups water. Bring to a boil over high heat. Cover the pot and decrease the heat to low. Simmer for 15 minutes, or until the liquid has been absorbed and the rice is tender.
- Remove from the heat and fluff the cooked rice with a fork.

### 4. Broil the marinated salmon or chicken ★★★

- Adjust the top oven rack to 6 inches below the broiler. Preheat the broiler to high.
- Cover a baking sheet with aluminum foil and lightly grease it with olive oil.
- Transfer the salmon or chicken with the marinade onto the baking sheet. Note: Be careful; make sure the marinade does not overflow.
- Broil for 3 minutes per side, or until dark brown and slightly charred.
- Carefully switch the baking sheet to the bottom rack and broil for an additional 3 to 7 minutes, or until the salmon or chicken is just cooked through. Note: Chicken will take 2 to 3 minutes longer to cook than salmon.

### 5. Sauté the spinach ★★

- Rinse the spinach and trim off the ends.
- In a skillet, heat 1 tablespoon of sesame oil over medium-high heat until hot.
- Add the spinach, 1 tablespoon water, and a pinch of salt and pepper to taste. Stir well.
- Cover the pan with a lid and steam for 2 minutes.

### 6. Serve your dish ★

- Place the broiled salmon or chicken on plates, drizzle with some of the sauce, sprinkle with the remaining scallions, and top with half of the Nori Sesame.
- Serve with the rice and sautéed spinach and sprinkle the remaining Nori Sesame over the top.

# Breaded and Fried Pork or Chicken, Cabbage, and Potato Salad
## Katsuretsu

**SERVES**
4

**ALLERGENS**
Dairy-Free, Nut-Free

**TOTAL PREP & COOK TIME**
1 hour

Often called simply katsu, katsuretsu (kaht-soo-RET-su) comes from the English word "cutlet" and was introduced in Ginza, Tokyo, as a Westernized meal way back in 1899. It is either served as a single dish or in combination with curry and generally includes shredded cabbage. It is traditionally prepared with pork cutlets, but chicken is also a great alternative.

## What You'll Need

1½ pounds pork or chicken cutlets

3 Yukon Gold potatoes

1 small cucumber

½ small head green cabbage

1 carrot

4 scallions (optional)

1 teaspoon sushi rice wine vinegar or apple cider vinegar

¼ cup mayonnaise

1½ teaspoons salt, plus more as needed

1 teaspoon pepper, plus more as needed

1 hard-boiled egg, peeled (optional)

¼ cup all-purpose flour

2 eggs

1 cup panko or breadcrumbs

3 tablespoons olive oil

1 tablespoon sesame seeds (optional)

### KETCHY TONKATSU SAUCE

⅓ cup tomato ketchup

2 tablespoons Worcestershire sauce

1 tablespoon soy sauce

1 tablespoon mirin

1 tablespoon sugar

¼ teaspoon Dijon mustard

¼ teaspoon garlic powder

1. **Prep the ingredients** ★★
- **Pork or chicken cutlets**—Thinly slice.
- **Potatoes**—Peel and cut into ½-inch cubes. Place them in a pot and cover with salted water.
- **Cucumber**—Cut into ¼-inch cubes.
- **Green cabbage**—Remove the core and thinly slice.
- **Carrot**—Peel and grate. Use half in step 2 and half in step 5.
- **Scallions (optional)**—Trim the ends and thinly slice.
- **Ketchy Tonkatsu Sauce**—Combine all the ingredients in a small bowl and mix well.

2. **Prep the Japanese potato salad** ★★
- Bring the saucepan with potatoes to a boil over medium-high heat. Lower the heat and cook until the potatoes are soft, 10 to 15 minutes. Drain them in a colander and return them to the saucepan.
- Add the sushi rice wine vinegar or apple cider vinegar to the cooked potatoes and lightly mash with a fork.
- Add half the shredded carrots and the cucumber, mayonnaise, and scallions (optional). Add salt and pepper to taste. Chop the boiled egg and add it to the mixture (optional).
- Transfer the mixture to a serving bowl and refrigerate while preparing the katsu.

3. **Prep the katsu** ★
- Season the pork or chicken cutlets with 1 teaspoon of salt and the pepper.
- Set up a breading station in this order: Bowl 1—Combine the flour with a pinch of salt and pepper; bowl 2—Whisk the eggs with 1 tablespoon cold water; bowl 3—Add the panko or breadcrumbs. Using tongs, dip the pork or chicken slices one at a time into the flour, then the egg (dripping off any excess back into the bowl), and finally in the panko or breadcrumbs. Use your hands to press the panko evenly onto both sides of the pork or chicken.
- Place the breaded pork or chicken on a plate or baking sheet.

4. **Cook the katsu** ★★★
- In a large skillet, heat 2 tablespoons of olive oil over medium-high heat until hot.
- Add the breaded pork or chicken in one even layer, being careful not to overcrowd the pan (cook in batches if necessary). Cook until crisp, golden brown, and cooked through, 4 to 5 minutes on each side, adding more oil if the pan begins to look dry.
- Place the cooked pork or chicken on a clean platter or plate.

5. **Sauté the vegetables** ★★
- In a large skillet, heat the remaining 1 tablespoon of olive oil over medium-high heat. Add the cabbage, remaining shredded carrots, remaining ½ teaspoon of salt, and pepper to taste.
- Cover the skillet and cook, stirring often, until the cabbage and carrots are tender, 5 to 6 minutes.

6. **Serve your dish** ★
- Place the pork or chicken katsu on plates, top with the Ketchy Tonkatsu Sauce, and sprinkle with the sesame seeds (optional). Serve with the sautéed cabbage and Japanese potato salad.

# Japanese Cabbage Pancakes with Mayo and Bonito Flakes
## Okonomiyaki

**SERVES**
4

**ALLERGENS**
Dairy-Free, Nut-Free

**TOTAL PREP & COOK TIME**
50 minutes

Okonomiyaki (oh-koh-noh-mee-YAH-kee) means "grilled as you like it" in Japanese. This savory pancake is traditionally made with shredded cabbage and various meats and is topped with condiments like scallions and bonito flakes (dried fish). Okonomiyaki is mainly associated with the Kansai or Hiroshima areas of Japan. Try to get mayonnaise in a squeeze bottle, which makes it easy to drizzle.

### What You'll Need

1 cup all-purpose flour

¼ teaspoon salt

¼ teaspoon sugar

¼ teaspoon baking powder

½ small head green cabbage

8 ounces bacon (optional)

3 scallions

3 eggs

1 tablespoon vegetable oil

½ cup mayonnaise

1 cup bonito flakes (optional)

### HOMEY OKONOMIYAKI SAUCE

¼ cup tomato ketchup

3 tablespoons Worcestershire sauce

2 tablespoons sugar

1 tablespoon oyster sauce

### 1. Prep the batter ★

- In a large bowl, combine 1 cup of all-purpose flour, ¼ teaspoon of salt, ¼ teaspoon of sugar, ¼ teaspoon of baking powder, and 1 cup water and stir until combined. The batter should be able to coat a spoon. If it is too thick, slowly add water, 1 tablespoon at a time.
- Cover with plastic wrap and let it rest in the refrigerator for at least 15 minutes while you prepare the other ingredients.

### 2. Prep the ingredients ★★

- Preheat the oven to 250°F.
- **Green cabbage**—Remove the core and finely chop, using a food processor, box grater, or sharp knife.
- **Bacon (optional)**—Cut the strips in half.
- **Scallions**—Trim the ends and thinly slice. Use half in step 3 and half in step 5.
- **Homey Okonomiyaki Sauce**—Combine all the ingredients in a small bowl and mix well.

### 3. Prep the okonomiyaki ★

- Remove the batter from the refrigerator.
- Add the eggs, cabbage, and half the sliced scallions and mix well until the cabbage is fully coated.

### 4. Cook the okonomiyaki ★★

- In a large nonstick skillet or pancake griddle, heat 1 tablespoon of vegetable oil over medium-high heat until hot.
- Spoon the okonomiyaki batter into the skillet to form 6-inch pancakes about ¾ inch thick.
- Place 2 or 3 slices of bacon on top of each okonomiyaki and cook until nicely browned, about 5 minutes. Gently flip and cook until nicely browned, about 5 minutes. Keep warm in the oven while completing the next batch of pancakes.

### 5. Serve your dish ★

- Spread the Homey Okonomiyaki Sauce on the bacon-covered side of the okonomiyaki.
- Drizzle the mayonnaise in zig-zagging lines if you have a squeeze bottle or spread it on with a knife, and sprinkle with the bonito flakes (optional).
- Garnish with the remaining scallions.

# China

China is the largest country in the world by population (1.4 billion), the third largest by land mass, and its history can be traced back to 1250 BCE. China is divided into 31 provinces and each province has its own unique food, dialect, and culture.

慢慢吃
màn màn chī
(mahn mahn chee)
*"Slowly enjoy!" in Chinese*

## YOU'LL COOK:

**Sesame-Ginger Meatballs Wrapped in Lettuce with Rice and Bok Choy (Ròu Wán)**

**Tofu with Ground Pork or Chicken and Steamed Rice (Mapo Tofu)**

**General Tso's Chicken with Sugar Snap Peas and Jasmine Rice (Zuo Zontang Ji)**

## DID YOU KNOW...

- The Great Wall of China is the largest man-made structure in the world (5,500 miles). The mortar used to bind the Great Wall's stones was made with sticky rice!

- China is about the same size as the United States, but it has only one official time zone.

- The first emperor of China (who started the Great Wall project) constructed a massive tomb for himself near the ancient city of Xi'an in Shaanxi province. The tomb is guarded by 8,000 life-size terra-cotta warriors, which took 37 years to make.

恭喜发财

吉祥如意

# Sesame-Ginger Meatballs Wrapped in Lettuce with Rice and Bok Choy
## Ròu Wán

These Asian-inspired chicken meatballs (roh WAHN) have become a fan favorite! To make it easier, healthier, and faster than the traditional way of frying, we broil the meatballs and braise them in a soy-sesame-ginger sauce. The secret ingredient to make the flavors pop? A bit of sugar! Served with Chinese bok choy, the meatballs can be eaten wrapped in a piece of lettuce like a taco or with rice on the side.

 **SERVES**
4

 **ALLERGENS**
Dairy-Free, Nut-Free

 **TOTAL PREP & COOK TIME**
50 minutes

## What You'll Need

4 garlic cloves

4 scallions

6 ounces button or cremini mushrooms

½ head butter lettuce

8 ounces bok choy or broccoli

1½ cups jasmine rice

1½ teaspoons salt, plus more as needed

1 tablespoon plus 1 teaspoon olive oil, plus more for greasing the baking sheet

1½ pounds ground chicken, pork, or turkey

1 large egg

1 cup panko or breadcrumbs

2 tablespoons plus 1 teaspoon sugar

1½ teaspoons cornstarch

1 tablespoon white sesame seeds (optional)

### GINGERLY SOY MIX

¾ cup Chinese rice wine (Shaoxing wine)

2 tablespoons soy sauce

1½ tablespoons oyster sauce

1 tablespoon sesame seeds

2 teaspoons vinegar

2 teaspoons ground ginger

1 teaspoon Dijon mustard

1 teaspoon sesame oil

### 1. Prep the ingredients ★ ★

- **Garlic**—Peel and mince or crush using a garlic press. Use half in step 3 and half in step 5.
- **Scallions**—Trim the ends and cut them into ⅛-inch slices. Reserve 1 tablespoon for garnishing in step 6.
- **Mushrooms**—Cut them into quarters.
- **Lettuce**—Wash and separate the leaves.
- **Bok choy or broccoli**—Wash and separate the bok choy leaves or cut the broccoli into florets.
- **Gingerly Soy Mix**—Combine all the ingredients in a small bowl and mix well.

### 2. Cook the rice ★ ★

- Rinse the rice in a colander to remove excess starch.
- In a small pot, combine the rice, a pinch of salt, and 2¼ cups water. Bring the water to a boil over medium-high heat.
- Decrease the heat, cover, and simmer until the liquid has been absorbed and the rice is tender, about 15 minutes. Remove from the heat, fluff the cooked rice with a fork, and keep warm until ready to serve.

### 3. Prep the chicken meatballs ★

- Lightly grease a baking sheet with olive oil.
- In a large bowl, combine the ground chicken, pork, or turkey, egg, panko or breadcrumbs, half the minced garlic, half the scallions, 2 tablespoons of sugar, and 1 teaspoon of salt. Using clean hands, gently mix them together.
- Form the mixture into 1-inch meatballs (you can use a small ice cream scoop!). Place them on the lightly greased baking sheet.

Continued...

# Sesame-Ginger Meatballs Wrapped in Lettuce with Rice and Bok Choy

## Ròu Wán

### 4. Broil and braise the meatballs ★★★

- In a bowl, mix 1½ teaspoons of cornstarch with 1 cup water.

- Adjust the top oven rack to 6 inches below the broiler. Preheat the broiler to high.

- Broil the meatballs until they are golden brown and cooked through, about 8 minutes. Be sure to keep an eye on them the entire time to prevent burning!

- In a Dutch oven or large pot, heat 1 tablespoon of olive oil over medium-high heat. Add the mushrooms and cook until they release their liquid. Add the meatballs, Gingerly Soy Mix, corn-starch mixture, and the remaining 1 teaspoon of sugar. Cover the pot, lower the heat to a simmer, and braise the meatballs, stirring occasionally, for about 10 min-utes. Taste, and if necessary, add some water to get the desired consistency.

### 5. Sauté the bok choy or broccoli (while the meatballs simmer) ★★

- In a large nonstick skillet, heat the remaining 1 teaspoon of olive oil over medium-high heat until hot.

- Add the remaining garlic, bok choy or broccoli, and remaining ½ teaspoon of salt. Cover the skillet and cook, stirring occasionally, until the vegetables are tender and the color is bright green, 3 to 5 minutes.

### 6. Serve your dish ★

- Spoon rice onto the lettuce leaves, top with the meatballs, and serve with the sautéed bok choy or broc-coli on the side.

- Garnish the meatballs with the remaining sliced scallions and sesame seeds (optional).

## DID YOU KNOW...

The Chinese are credited with the "Four Great Inventions" that greatly influenced human civilization: papermaking, printing, gunpowder, and the compass.

# Tofu with Ground Pork or Chicken and Steamed Rice
## Mapo Tofu

Mapo tofu (MAH-poh DOH-foo) was apparently named after a cook from Chengdu, the capital of Sichuan province, because his face was disfigured with scars and he looked like an old woman. The word "ma" stands for "ma-zi," meaning pockmarks, and "po" stands for "popo," an old lady. This meal is slightly spicy and savory, which goes well with steamed rice.

 **SERVES**
4

 **ALLERGENS**
Dairy-Free, Nut-Free

 **TOTAL PREP & COOK TIME**
30 minutes

### What You'll Need

3 garlic cloves

4 scallions

1½ cups jasmine rice

Salt

1 tablespoon cornstarch

1 tablespoon oil

1½ pounds ground pork or ground chicken

1 teaspoon sugar

1 (16-oz) package medium-firm tofu

### MAPOT SAUCE MIX

2½ tablespoons soy sauce

1½ tablespoons Chinese rice wine (Shaoxing wine)

1½ tablespoons spicy fermented bean paste

1 teaspoon chicken bouillon

1 teaspoon sugar

1 teaspoon sesame oil

½ teaspoon Chinese five-spice powder

### 1. Prep the ingredients ★★

- **Garlic**—Peel and mince or crush using a garlic press.
- **Scallions**—Trim the ends and cut into ⅛-inch slices.
- **MapoT Sauce Mix**—Combine all the ingredients in a small bowl and mix well.

### 2. Cook the rice ★★

- Rinse the rice in a colander to remove excess starch.
- In a small pot, combine the rice, a pinch of salt, and 2¼ cups water.
- Bring to a boil over medium-high heat.
- Decrease the heat to low, cover, and simmer until the liquid has been absorbed and the rice is tender, about 15 minutes.
- Remove from the heat, fluff the cooked rice with a fork, and keep warm until ready to serve.

### 3. Stir-fry the pork or chicken ★★★

- In a bowl, mix 1 tablespoon of cornstarch with 1 cup water.
- In a large skillet, heat 1 tablespoon of oil over medium-high heat until hot.
- Add the ground pork or chicken, using a fork to break up the meat. Stir-fry until browned, about 5 minutes. Add the garlic and cook until fragrant, about 2 minutes.
- Lower the heat, add the MapoT Sauce Mix, the cornstarch mixture, and 1 teaspoon of sugar and simmer for 2 minutes.
- Taste and, if necessary, add water 1 tablespoon at a time to get the desired consistency.

### 4. Complete the dish and serve ★★

- Gently slide the tofu cubes and scallions into the skillet and stir gently. Simmer until the tofu absorbs the flavors, about 5 minutes.
- Divide the rice among individual plates and serve with stir-fry on the side.

# General Tso's Chicken with Sugar Snap Peas and Jasmine Rice
## Zuo Zontang Ji

**SERVES**
4

**ALLERGENS**
Dairy-Free, Nut-Free

**TOTAL PREP & COOK TIME**
50 minutes

This sweet and salty deep-fried chicken (Zuo Zontang Ji) is often served at Chinese restaurants in the United States. Originating from Hunan province in China, it is rumored to be named after Zuo Zongtang, a military leader during the Qing dynasty. Whether General Zuo (also spelled Tso) really ate this dish, nobody knows, but we're lucky to have the recipe now!

## What You'll Need

2 garlic cloves

4 scallions

1 pound sugar snap peas

1 large egg

2 pounds boneless skinless chicken tenders or chicken thighs

1½ cups jasmine rice

½ teaspoon salt, plus more as needed

1½ teaspoons olive oil, plus more as needed

½ cup all-purpose flour

¼ cup plus 1½ teaspoons cornstarch

½ teaspoon baking powder

2 tablespoons sugar

1 tablespoon sesame seeds (optional)

### GENTSO SAUCE

¼ cup Chinese rice wine (Shaoxing wine)

2½ tablespoons Chinese black rice vinegar

2 tablespoons dark soy sauce

1 teaspoon granulated garlic

1 teaspoon ground ginger

1 teaspoon sesame oil

### 1. Prep the ingredients ★★

- Preheat the oven to 450°F.
- **Garlic**—Peel and mince or crush using a garlic press.
- **Scallions**—Trim the ends and cut into ⅛-inch slices.
- **Sugar snap peas**—Trim the ends.
- **Egg**—Separate the yolk from the white. Save the yolk for another use.
- **Chicken**—Cut into ½-inch pieces.
- **GenTso Sauce**—Combine all the ingredients in a small bowl and mix well.

### 2. Prep the marinade ★★

- In a large bowl, beat the egg white until light and foamy.
- Add ¼ cup of the GenTso Sauce (save the rest for step 5) and whisk well to combine.
- Add the chicken pieces to the marinade, turn to coat evenly, and set aside on a plate.

### 3. Cook the rice ★★

- Rinse the rice in a colander to remove excess starch.
- In a small pot, combine the rice, a pinch of salt, and 2¼ cups water. Bring to a boil over medium-high heat.
- Decrease the heat to low, cover, and simmer until the liquid has been absorbed and the rice is tender, about 15 minutes.
- Remove from the heat, fluff the cooked rice with a fork, and keep warm until ready to serve.

### 4. Bake the chicken ★★★

- Lightly grease a baking sheet with olive oil.
- In a bowl, combine the flour, ¼ cup of cornstarch, ½ teaspoon of baking powder, and ½ teaspoon of salt and mix well.
- Add the chicken pieces to the flour mixture and turn to evenly coat—press firmly so the dry mixture sticks. Place the chicken pieces on the prepared baking sheet; do not overcrowd.
- Bake until the chicken is lightly browned, 10 to 12 minutes. Turn the chicken and cook until browned on the other side, 10 to 12 more minutes.

### 5. Finish the chicken with the sauce ★★★

- In a bowl, combine the remaining GenTso Sauce, remaining 1½ teaspoons cornstarch, ½ cup water, and 2 tablespoons of sugar and stir well.
- In a large skillet, heat 1½ teaspoons of olive oil over medium-high heat until hot. Add the scallions and minced garlic and sauté until aromatic, about 1 minute.
- Slowly add the sauce mix and stir well until it boils and thickens, about 1 minute.
- Add the crispy chicken pieces and toss until all pieces are thoroughly coated with sauce.

### 6. Cook the sugar snap peas and serve your dish ★★

- Bring a medium pot filled with salted water to a boil. Add the sugar snap peas and cook until crisp-tender, 1 to 2 minutes. Using a colander, drain the sugar snap peas.
- Divide the chicken among individual plates and garnish with the sesame seeds (optional). Serve immediately with the steamed rice and sugar snap peas.

# India

India is the second largest country in the world by population (1.37 billion) and seventh largest by land mass, and its history can be traced back to 1500 BCE. It was colonized by the British for almost 200 years from 1757 to 1947.

भोजन का आन?द लें
Bhojan ka Anand len
(bho-jan ka a-nand le)
*"Enjoy your food" in Hindi*

**YOU'LL COOK:**

**Meatballs in Curry with Naan and Sautéed Cabbage (Kofta Curry)**

**Vegetables Braised in a Spiced Coconut Sauce with Basmati Rice (Navratan Korma)**

**Coconut Curry with Chicken or Tofu, Naan, and Roasted Cauliflower (Nilgiri Korma)**

- The board game Snakes and Ladders, also commonly known as Chutes and Ladders, originally came from ancient India. The game was translated into English and transported to the United Kingdom in the 19th century during colonial times.

- About 70 percent of the world's spices come from India!

- India is home to one of the Seven Wonders of the World—the Taj Mahal. It was built by Mughal emperor Shah Jahan in 1632 in memory of his wife. The people of India think of it as a symbol of eternal love.

# Meatballs in Curry with Naan and Sautéed Cabbage
## Kofta Curry

From the Persian "kūfta," meaning pounded meat, kofta are spiced meatballs or meatloaf dishes found in Middle Eastern and South and Central Asian cuisines. This kofta meatball curry in a tomato masala sauce is from the state of Goa, on the western coast of the Indian peninsula.

**SERVES**
4

**ALLERGENS**
Dairy-Free, Nut-Free, Gluten-Free Optional, Vegetarian Optional

**TOTAL PREP & COOK TIME**
45 minutes

### What You'll Need

1 medium onion

½ medium head cabbage

2 tablespoons olive oil, plus more as needed

1½ pounds ground beef or ground chicken

1 egg

1¾ teaspoons salt

¼ cup breadcrumbs (optional)

1 (15-oz) can crushed tomatoes

1 cup plain yogurt

½ teaspoon sugar

4 pieces naan or gluten-free pita bread

### Vegetarian Option

3 medium zucchini

½ cup chickpea flour

### KA'KOFTA CURRY MIX

2 teaspoons ground cumin

2 teaspoons garam masala

1½ teaspoons curry powder

1 teaspoon ground coriander

1 teaspoon ground ginger

½ teaspoon paprika

1 cinnamon stick

1 bay leaf

1 curry leaf

### BANDH GOBI

½ teaspoon mustard seed

½ teaspoon ground turmeric

### 1. Prep the ingredients ★★

- Preheat the oven to the lowest setting.
- **Onion**—Peel and finely dice. Use half in step 2 and half in step 3.
- **Cabbage**—Cut out and discard the core and thinly slice.
- **Ka'kofta Curry Mix**—Combine all the ingredients in a small bowl and mix well.
- **Bandh Gobi**—Combine all the ingredients in a small bowl and mix well.

**Vegetarian option**

- **Zucchini**—Trim the ends. Grate, wrap it in paper towels, and squeeze out as much liquid as possible. In a large bowl, combine the zucchini with the chickpea flour (add more chickpea flour, 1 tablespoon at a time, if the mixture is too wet).

### 2. Prep the meatballs ★

- Lightly grease a baking sheet with olive oil.
- In a large bowl, combine the ground meat or zucchini mixture, egg, 1 teaspoon of the Ka'kofta Curry Mix, half the diced onion, ½ teaspoon of salt, and the bread-crumbs (optional). Using clean hands, gently mix together.
- Form the mixture into 1½-inch meatballs (you can use a small ice cream scoop!). Place them on the lightly greased baking sheet.

### 3. Prep the kofta curry ★★★

- Adjust the top oven rack to 6 inches below the broiler. Preheat the broiler to high.
- Broil the meatballs until golden brown, 8 to 10 minutes. Be sure to keep an eye on them the entire time so they don't burn!
- In a Dutch oven or large pot, heat 1 tablespoon of the olive oil over medium-high heat.
- Add the remaining onion and the remaining Ka'kofta Curry Mix. Stir continuously until fragrant, 3 to 5 minutes. Add the meatballs, crushed tomatoes, yogurt, sugar, 1 teaspoon of salt, and 1 cup water and stir slowly to mix well.
- Lower the heat and let simmer for 15 minutes (do not stir).

### 4. Sauté the cabbage (while the kofta is simmering) ★★

- In a skillet, heat the remaining 1 tablespoon of olive oil over medium-high heat.
- Add the Bandh Gobi mix and cover the skillet.
- When the mustard seeds stop popping, 1 to 2 minutes, add the cabbage and remaining ¼ teaspoon of salt. Cover the skillet and cook until the cabbage is tender, 5 to 6 minutes.

### 5. Reheat the naan ★

- Brush the naan or gluten-free pita with olive oil. Place on a rimmed baking sheet and warm in the oven for 3 to 4 minutes until warm and pliable (or place the naan on a microwave-safe plate and microwave for 15 seconds).

### 6. Serve your dish ★

- Place the kofta meatballs and spiced cabbage onto plates and serve with the warm naan or gluten-free pita on the side.

# Vegetables Braised in a Spiced Coconut Sauce with Basmati Rice
## Navratan Korma

This creamy and flavorful curry was created in the imperial kitchens during the Mughal Empire's medieval period (1526–1707). Their dishes had a great influence on Northern Indian, Bangladeshi, and Pakistani cuisines. The word "navratan" means "nine gems," which represents the nine different vegetables, fruits, and nuts used to cook the curry.

 **SERVES**
4

 **ALLERGENS**
Dairy-Free, Nut-Free, Gluten-Free, Vegetarian

 **TOTAL PREP & COOK TIME**
30 minutes

## What You'll Need

1 medium yellow onion

1 medium potato

2 carrots

3 ounces green beans

¼ head cauliflower

2 cups basmati or other long-grain rice

1 teaspoon salt, plus more as needed

1 tablespoon olive oil

1 cup frozen peas

1 teaspoon tomato paste

3 tablespoons cashew butter or peanut butter

½ cup plain yogurt

1 (15-oz) can coconut milk

1 teaspoon sugar

Pepper

### KORMA SPICE MIX

1 tablespoon ground cashews

1 teaspoon curry powder

1 teaspoon ground cumin

1 teaspoon ground coriander

1 teaspoon garlic powder

1 teaspoon salt

1 teaspoon ground ginger

½ teaspoon garam masala

½ teaspoon chili powder

¼ teaspoon ground cinnamon

¼ teaspoon ground turmeric

### 1. Prep the ingredients ★★

- **Onion**—Peel and dice.
- **Potato**—Peel and cut into ½-inch cubes. Put in a bowl and cover with water until step 3.
- **Carrots**—Peel and cut into ½-inch rounds.
- **Green beans**—Trim and discard the ends. Cut into 1-inch pieces.
- **Cauliflower**—Trim the end and cut the florets and stem into 1-inch pieces.
- **Korma Spice Mix**—Combine all the ingredients in a small bowl and mix well.

### 2. Cook the basmati rice ★★

- Rinse the rice in a colander to remove excess starch.
- In a small pot, combine the rice, a pinch of salt, and 2½ cups water. Bring to a boil over medium-high heat.
- Decrease the heat to low, cover, and simmer until the liquid has been absorbed and the rice is tender, about 15 minutes. Remove from the heat and fluff the cooked rice with a fork.

### 3. Prep the vegetable korma ★★

- In a Dutch oven or heavy-bottomed pot, heat 1 tablespoon of olive oil over medium-high heat until hot.
- Add the Korma Spice Mix and diced onion and sauté, stirring continuously until fragrant, 2 to 3 minutes.
- Drain the potatoes and add them to the pot.
- Add the carrots, cauliflower, green beans, peas, tomato paste, cashew butter or peanut butter, yogurt, coconut milk, 1 cup water, 1 teaspoon of sugar , and 1 teaspoon of salt and stir well.
- Lower the heat, cover, and simmer until the vegetables are tender, 8 to 10 minutes. Season with salt and pepper to taste.

### 4. Serve your dish ★

- Place a scoop of rice into individual bowls. Ladle the vegetable korma over the top.

# Coconut Curry with Chicken or Tofu, Naan, and Roasted Cauliflower
## Nilgiri Korma

You don't often see Indian green curry! This dish is from the hilly region of Nilgiris in the southern state of Tamil Nadu. The traditional version uses fresh coriander, mint, green chiles, and Indian spices. In ours, we omit the chiles to cut the spiciness. Feel free to add red pepper flakes if you like it hot!

**SERVES**
4

**ALLERGENS**
Dairy-Free, Nut-Free, Gluten-Free Optional, Vegetarian Optional

**TOTAL PREP & COOK TIME**
40 minutes

### What You'll Need

2 pounds boneless skinless chicken thighs or breasts

1 medium head cauliflower

1 onion

1 lime

1 tablespoon plus 1 teaspoon olive oil

1½ teaspoons salt

Pepper

1 (15-oz) can coconut milk

4 pieces naan or gluten-free pita bread

### Vegetarian Option

2 (16-oz) packages firm tofu

2 cups mixed frozen vegetables

### NILGIRI CURRY SPICE

¼ cup dried cilantro

2 teaspoons ground ginger

2 teaspoons dried mint

1 teaspoon ground turmeric

1 teaspoon ground coriander

1 teaspoon garlic powder

½ teaspoon sugar

¼ teaspoon ground cinnamon

### 1. Prep the ingredients ★★

- Preheat the oven to 400°F.
- **Chicken**—Trim the fat and cut into 1½- to 2-inch cubes.
- **Cauliflower**—Trim the ends and discard. Cut the head into small florets and the stem into strips.
- **Onion**—Peel and dice.
- **Lime**—Halve and juice.
- **Nilgiri Curry Spice**—Combine all the ingredients in a small bowl and mix well.

**Vegetarian option**

- **Tofu**—Drain. Use paper towels to press out the liquid from the tofu. Cut into 1-inch cubes.

### 2. Roast the cauliflower ★★

- Toss the cauliflower with ½ teaspoon of the Nilgiri Curry Spice, 1 tablespoon of olive oil, ½ teaspoon of salt, and pepper to taste in a large bowl. Spread the cauliflower evenly on a rimmed baking sheet.
- Bake, stirring occasionally, until the cauliflower is tender and golden brown, 20 to 25 minutes.

### 3. Prep the curry ★★★ (while the cauliflower is roasting)

- In a Dutch oven, heat the remaining 1 teaspoon of olive oil over medium-high heat until hot.
- Add the onion and remaining Nilgiri Curry Spice. Stir continuously until fragrant, 3 to 5 minutes.
- Add the chicken or the tofu and mixed vegetables, the remaining 1 teaspoon of salt, and pepper to taste and sauté until the chicken or vegetables begin to brown, about 5 minutes.

### 4. Simmer the curry ★★★

- Add the coconut milk and lime juice and stir until combined. Bring to a simmer, cover with a lid, and cook until the chicken is tender, 15 to 20 minutes.
- Remove the lid and bring to a boil to concentrate the liquid, 3 to 5 minutes, or until the desired consistency is reached.

### 5. Warm the naan ★★

- Arrange the naan or gluten-free pita bread on a baking sheet and warm in the oven for 3 to 4 minutes until warm and pliable (or place on a microwave-safe plate and microwave for 15 seconds).

### 6. Serve your dish ★

- Spoon the curry into a big bowl and serve it alongside the warm naan or gluten-free pita bread and roasted cauliflower.

# Singapore

Singapore was founded in 1819 by Sir Stamford Raffles and it became a British colony. It was part of the Independent Federation of Malaya (Malaysia) until its independence on August 9, 1965. The British established the legal system, education system, and infrastructure.

Selamat Menjamu Selera
(se-lah-mat men-ja-moo se-le-ra)
*"Please eat!" in Malay*

**YOU'LL COOK:**

**Skewered Chicken with Rice, Peanut Dipping Sauce, and Pickled Cucumber (Singapore Satay)**

**Soy Chicken with Chinese Broccoli in Garlic Sauce with Rice (Singapore Chicken Rice)**

**Fried Rice Noodles with Shrimp and Summer Vegetables (Singapore Bee Hoon)**

- Singapore is one of only three surviving city-states in the world. The other two are Monaco and Vatican City.

- Singapore is not only one island—it actually has 63 islands dotted around one main island!

- The country's name of "Singapore" comes from the Sanskrit name "Singapura," which means "lion city."

# Skewered Chicken with Rice, Peanut Dipping Sauce, and Pickled Cucumber
## Singapore Satay

**SERVES**
4

**ALLERGENS**
Dairy-Free, Gluten-Free

**TOTAL PREP & COOK TIME**
1 hour + 2 hours or up to overnight to marinate

Satay (skewered grilled spiced meat) is a well-known Southeast Asian–style dish. Though Indonesia is thought to be its true birthplace, this dish is found in Thailand, Malaysia, and Singapore. Chicken, pork, or beef is marinated overnight to fully absorb the flavors, skewered onto wooden or bamboo sticks, and grilled over charcoal. Serve it with homemade peanut dipping sauce, cucumber, and a bowl of rice.

## What You'll Need

15 to 20 (6-inch) wooden skewers

2 pounds boneless skinless chicken thighs or pork tenderloin

2 cucumbers

1 lime

2 tablespoons fish sauce or Worcestershire sauce

3 tablespoons olive oil, plus more as needed

1½ cups jasmine rice

½ teaspoon salt, plus more as needed

1 tablespoon plus 2 teaspoons sugar

1 tablespoon white vinegar or apple cider vinegar

½ cup creamy peanut butter

2 tablespoons hoisin sauce

**G'DAY SATAY MIX**

3 tablespoons brown sugar

1 tablespoon lemongrass powder

2 teaspoons ground ginger

1½ teaspoons ground turmeric

1 teaspoon ground coriander

1 teaspoon garlic powder

1 teaspoon onion powder

½ teaspoon chili powder

### 1. Prep the ingredients ★★

- **Wooden skewers**—Submerge in water fully and soak for at least 10 minutes.
- **Chicken thighs or pork tenderloin**—Remove the fat and cut into 1-inch cubes.
- **Cucumbers**—Trim the ends. Cut in half lengthwise and cut into ¼-inch half-moons. Soak the cut cucumbers in cold water.
- **Lime**—Halve and juice.
- **G'day Satay Mix**—Combine all the ingredients in a large bowl and mix well.

### 2. Prep the satay marinade ★

- Add the fish sauce or Worcestershire sauce and 2 tablespoons of olive oil to the G'day Satay Mix and stir until it becomes a paste.
- Add the chicken or pork pieces to the marinade and stir well to combine. Note: If time allows, marinate the chicken pieces for at least 2 hours or overnight to maximize the flavors.

### 3. Cook the rice ★★

- Rinse the rice in a colander to remove excess starch.
- In a small pot, combine the rice, a pinch of salt, and 2¼ cups water and bring to a boil over high heat.
- Decrease the heat to low, cover, and simmer until the liquid has been absorbed and the rice is tender, about 15 minutes. Remove from the heat and fluff the rice with a fork.

### 4. Prep the pickled cucumber and peanut dipping sauce ★

- In a bowl, whisk remaining 1 tablespoon of oil, ½ teaspoon of salt, 2 teaspoons of sugar, and 1 tablespoon of white vinegar or apple cider vinegar. Drain the sliced cucumber, add to the bowl, and toss until combined. Let sit for at least 15 minutes.
- In a bowl, combine the creamy peanut butter, hoisin sauce, 2 teaspoons of lime juice, 2 tablespoons water, and remaining 1 tablespoon of sugar. Whisk well to fully combine the ingredients. If necessary, add water, 1 tablespoon at a time, to get the desired consistency.

### 5. Prep the chicken satay ★★★

- Remove the skewers from the water. Place 4 or 5 pieces of marinated chicken or pork on each skewer. Brush the chicken or pork with olive oil and place the skewers on a rimmed baking sheet.
- Adjust the top oven rack to 6 inches below the broiler. Preheat the broiler to high.
- Broil the skewers until the meat is dark and golden brown, 3 to 4 minutes. Carefully flip the skewers and broil until cooked through, another 3 to 4 minutes.

### 6. Serve your dish ★

- Place the satay skewers on a platter and serve with the rice, pickled cucumber, and peanut dipping sauce.

# Soy Chicken with Chinese Broccoli in Garlic Sauce with Rice
## Singapore Chicken Rice

Adapted by Chinese immigrants from Hainan province in southern China, this dish is a must-try for visitors to Singapore and fans of Asian cuisine! It is a popular street food and can be found in hawker centers, food courts, and restaurants throughout Singapore. The chicken is poached in a soy, garlic, and ginger marinade, while the rice is infused with chicken broth.

**SERVES**
4

**ALLERGENS**
Dairy-Free, Nut-Free

**TOTAL PREP & COOK TIME**
1 hour

## What You'll Need

6 scallions

8 ounces kai-lan (Chinese broccoli) or regular broccoli

2 garlic cloves

4 bone-in chicken legs or 2 pounds boneless thighs

1½ cups jasmine rice

1 teaspoon salt, plus more as needed

2¼ cups chicken stock

1 tablespoon plus 1 teaspoon olive oil

2 teaspoons oyster sauce

½ teaspoon sesame oil

½ teaspoon sugar

1 teaspoon cornstarch

### HONEYIN' SOY SAUCE

⅓ cup soy sauce

2 tablespoons dark soy sauce

2 tablespoons Chinese rice wine (Shaoxing wine)

2 tablespoons honey

1 tablespoon garlic powder

2 teaspoons ground ginger

2 star anise pods

1 cinnamon stick

1. **Prep** ★★
- **Scallions**— ...nds. Cut 4 scallions into ... .ch slices for step 2. Thinly slice 2 scallions for step 5.
- **Kai-lan**—Trim the ends. OR **Broccoli**—Trim the ends and cut into florets.
- **Garlic**—Mince.
- **Honeyin' Soy Sauce**—Combine all the ingredients in a small bowl and mix well.

2. **Braise the chicken** ★★★
- In a large pot over medium-high heat, combine the Honeyin' Soy Sauce, the 2-inch scallions, chicken legs or thighs, and 1 cup water. Bring to a boil and cook for 5 minutes.
- Lower the heat and simmer, using tongs to occasionally turn the chicken pieces, until the chicken is tender, about 30 minutes. Remove and discard the star anise pods and cinnamon stick.

3. **Cook the rice (while the chicken is cooking)** ★★
- Rinse the rice in a colander to remove excess starch.
- In a small pot, combine the rice, a pinch of salt, and the chicken stock.
- Bring to a boil over medium-high heat.
- Lower the heat, cover, and simmer for 15 minutes, or until the liquid has been absorbed and the rice is tender. Remove from the heat and fluff the cooked rice with a fork.

4. **Prep the kai-lan or broccoli (while the chicken is cooking)** ★★
- Fill a wok or large skillet with 1 inch of water, 1 tablespoon of olive oil, and 1 teaspoon of salt. Bring to a boil over medium-high heat.
- Gently add the kai-lan or broccoli to the boiling liquid and blanch for 2 to 3 minutes, or until they are bright green and crisp-tender.
- Using a colander, drain the kai-lan or broccoli and arrange it on a large serving platter. Keep warm until ready to serve.

5. **Prep the garlic sauce (while the chicken is cooking)** ★★
- In a bowl, combine the oyster sauce, sesame oil, ½ teaspoon of sugar, 1 tablespoon water, and 1 teaspoon of cornstarch.
- In the same wok or skillet, heat the remaining 1 teaspoon of olive oil over medium-high heat until hot.
- Add the minced garlic and sauté for 1 minute. Add the oyster sauce mixture and sliced scallions and cook over high heat for 30 seconds.
- Pour the sauce over the blanched kai-lan or broccoli.

6. **Serve your dish** ★
- Transfer the chicken pieces to the platter with the kai-lan or broccoli.
- Drizzle some Honeyin' Soy cooking liquid from the pot over the chicken and serve with the rice and kai-lan or broccoli in garlic sauce.

# Fried Rice Noodles with Shrimp and Summer Vegetables
## Singapore Bee Hoon

This quick and flavorful dish is often served for breakfast in Singapore! Rice noodles are soaked in boiling water and tossed with sautéed summer-fresh produce, sweet shrimp, and a savory sauce. Our sauce uses traditional ingredients such as soy sauce and rice wine, but we also added curry powder. Way better than take-out and far more healthy and delicious!

 **SERVES**
4

 **ALLERGENS**
Dairy-Free, Nut-Free

 **TOTAL PREP & COOK TIME**
30 minutes

## What You'll Need

1 medium onion

3 scallions

1 red bell pepper

5 ounces green beans

1 pound medium shrimp

9 ounces rice noodles or angel hair pasta

2 eggs

½ teaspoon salt, plus more as needed

2 tablespoons olive oil

½ teaspoon sugar

Pepper

## SINGAPORE CURRY MIX

3½ tablespoons soy sauce

2½ tablespoons Chinese rice wine (Shaoxing wine)

2½ teaspoons curry powder

2 teaspoons sugar

1 teaspoon granulated garlic

1. **Prep the ingredients** ⭐⭐
- **Onion**—Peel and thinly slice.
- **Scallions**—Trim the ends and cut into 2-inch slices.
- **Bell pepper**—Cut in half and discard the stem and seeds. Cut into ¼-inch strips.
- **Green beans**—Trim the ends and cut in half.
- **Shrimp**—Peel off the shell and remove the tail.
- **Singapore Curry Mix**—Combine all the ingredients in a small bowl and mix well.

2. **Prep the rice noodles or angel hair pasta** ⭐⭐
- Bring a large pot of water to a boil. Add the rice noodles or angel hair pasta and cook until al dente (firm to the bite but not overcooked), 4 to 5 minutes for rice noodles or 8 to 10 minutes for pasta.
- Drain in a colander and rinse with cold water to stop the cooking.

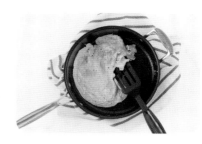

3. **Prep the omelet** ⭐⭐
- In a bowl, combine the eggs, 1 tablespoon water, and a pinch of salt and whisk well.
- In a large nonstick skillet, heat 1 tablespoon of olive oil over medium-high heat until hot. Add the egg mixture and cook the omelet until the bottom sets and is cooked through, 2 to 3 minutes.
- Carefully flip the omelet onto a cutting board and cut it into strips.

4. **Sauté the shrimp and vegetables** ⭐⭐
- In the same nonstick skillet, heat the remaining 1 tablespoon of olive oil over medium-high heat until hot.
- Add the onion, bell pepper, green beans, ½ teaspoon of salt, ½ teaspoon of sugar, and pepper to taste. Sauté for 5 to 6 minutes, until the vegetables are tender.
- Add the shrimp and cook until they are pink and cooked through evenly, about 3 minutes.
- Add the noodles, Singapore Curry Mix, scallions, ¼ cup water, and omelet strips to the skillet.
- Toss to combine and cook for 3 to 5 minutes, until heated through.

5. **Serve your dish** ⭐
- Transfer the noodles to serving plates.

# South Korea

South Korea (and North Korea) is on a peninsula attached to northeastern China that has records of inhabitants from as early as the 7th century BCE. South Korea is surrounded by three bodies of water (the Yellow Sea, the East Sea, and the East China Sea) and is made up of about 3,000 islands, mostly small and uninhabited.

맛있게 드세요!
Mas-issge deuseyo!
(mat-it-ge du-se-yo)
*"Enjoy your meal!" in Korean*

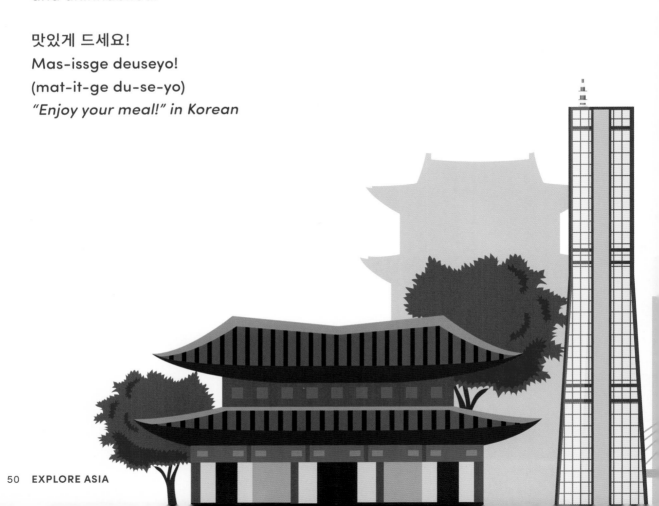

**YOU'LL COOK:**

**Korean BBQ Chicken with Side Dishes and Rice (Dak Bulgogi)**

**Korean Rolls with Ground Beef or Tofu (Bulgogi Kimbap)**

**Mung Bean Pancakes with Kimchi (Nokdu Bindaetteok)**

# Korean BBQ Chicken with Side Dishes and Rice
## Dak Bulgogi

**SERVES**
4

**ALLERGENS**
Dairy-Free, Nut-Free, Vegetarian Optional

**TOTAL PREP & COOK TIME**
50 minutes + 2 hours or up to overnight to marinate

"Bulgogi" literally means "fire meat," which in other words means "barbecue," something so popular in South Korea that if you find yourself at a Korean restaurant, you must try it. It is usually thinly sliced marinated beef, but we use chicken in our recipe, and instead of grilling it, we are broiling it. Namul is a kind of side dish (banchan). It is customary to have an assortment of banchan in traditional Korean cuisine.

### What You'll Need

1 Bosc pear or apple

4 garlic cloves

3 scallions

2 pounds boneless skinless chicken thighs or beef sirloin or tenderloin

1 bunch broccoli rabe or spinach

8 ounces radishes

½ head Bibb lettuce (optional)

1½ cups short-grain rice

2 teaspoons salt, plus more as needed

1 tablespoon olive oil, plus more as needed

2 tablespoons rice wine vinegar or apple cider vinegar

1 tablespoon fish sauce or Worcestershire sauce

1 tablespoon sugar

3 tablespoons sesame oil or olive oil

1 teaspoon granulated garlic

1½ teaspoons sesame seeds

Pepper

### Vegetarian Option

2 (16-oz) packages firm tofu

### DAKGOGI SAUCE

½ cup soy sauce

1½ tablespoons sugar

1 tablespoon mirin

1 tablespoon sesame oil

2 teaspoons Gochujang paste

1 teaspoon garlic powder

1. **Marinate the meat or tofu** ★ ★
   **(for at least 2 hours or overnight)**
- **Pear or apple**—Peel and grate the fruit using a grater.
- **Garlic**—Peel and mince.
- **Scallions**—Trim the ends and thinly slice.
- **Chicken thigh**—Remove any fat and cut into 2- to 3-inch pieces. OR **Beef**—Cut into thin slices; the thinner the better.
- **Dakgogi Sauce**—Combine all the ingredients in a small bowl and mix well.

**Vegetarian option**
- **Tofu**—Drain. Use paper towels to press out the liquid from the tofu. Cut into ½-inch slices.
- In a bowl, combine the Dakgogi Sauce, chicken or beef or tofu, minced garlic, grated pear or apple, and scallion and mix well. Let it marinate.

2. **Prep the ingredients** ★ ★
- **Broccoli rabe or spinach**—Rinse well. Trim the ends and roughly chop.
- **Radishes**—Trim the ends and cut into quarters.
- **Lettuce (optional)**—Rinse and separate the leaves.

3. **Cook the rice** ★ ★
- Rinse the rice in a colander to remove excess starch.
- In a small pot, combine the rinsed rice, a pinch of salt, and 2¼ cups water. Bring to a boil over medium-high heat.
- Lower the heat, cover, and simmer until the liquid has been absorbed and the rice is tender, about 15 minutes. Remove from the heat and fluff the cooked rice with a fork.

Continued...

# Korean BBQ Chicken with Side Dishes and Rice

## Dak Bulgogi

**4. Prep the radish salad and broccoli rabe (while the rice is cooking)** ★

- **Radish Salad**—In a bowl, whisk together 1 tablespoon of oil, 2 tablespoons of rice wine vinegar or apple cider vinegar, 1 tablespoon of fish sauce or Worcestershire sauce, 1 tablespoon of sugar, 1 tablespoon water, 1 teaspoon of salt, and 1 tablespoon of sesame oil. Add the cut radishes and toss until combined. Let sit for at least 15 minutes.

- **Broccoli Rabe**—Bring a deep skillet filled with water and the remaining 1 teaspoon of salt to a boil. Add the broccoli rabe or spinach and blanch for 30 seconds. Transfer to a bowl with ice-cold water to cool down and then drain using a colander. In a bowl, toss together the blanched broccoli rabe or spinach, 1 teaspoon of granulated garlic, 1½ teaspoons of sesame seeds, 2 tablespoons of sesame oil or olive oil, a pinch of salt, and pepper to taste.

**5. Broil the marinated meat or tofu** ★★★

- Adjust the top oven rack to 6 inches below the broiler. Preheat the broiler to high. Cover a baking sheet with aluminum foil and lightly grease with oil.

- Transfer the marinated meat or tofu with its marinade to the baking sheet. Note: Be careful. Make sure the marinade does not overflow.

- Broil for 3 to 5 minutes per side, or until the meat or tofu is dark brown and slightly charred. Carefully move the baking sheet to the bottom rack and cook for an additional 3 to 5 minutes, or until the meat or tofu is just cooked through. Note: Chicken will need an extra 2 to 3 minutes of cooking.

**6. Serve your dish** ★

- Place the meat or tofu on plates, drizzle with some sauce, and serve with the rice and the broccoli rabe or spinach and radish salad. As an alternative, serve with rice on lettuce leaves along with the side dishes.

## DID YOU KNOW...

Hangul is the Korean alphabet, created in the 15th century. It is considered one of the most scientific writing systems in the world. Hangul is easy to learn and has 14 consonants and 10 vowels, forming syllabic blocks.

# Korean Rolls with Ground Beef or Tofu
## Bulgogi Kimbap

Pronounced "GIM-bap," this is a Korean seaweed rice roll filled with vegetables. They are similar to Japanese sushi except the rice is not seasoned with vinegar. It is a tradition to make children kimbap for lunch or when they go on a school picnic or field trip in Korea. It is also a common street and party food. In this recipe we use bulgogi beef (Korean BBQ beef) and vegetables, but you can have fun trying out different fillings.

 **SERVES**
4

 **ALLERGENS**
Dairy-Free, Nut-Free, Vegetarian Optional

 **TOTAL PREP & COOK TIME**
50 minutes

## What You'll Need

5 radishes

1 cucumber

1 carrot

3 scallions

2 cups short-grain rice

½ teaspoon salt, plus more as needed

1 tablespoon soy sauce

1 tablespoon sesame oil, plus more as needed

1 tablespoon rice wine vinegar or apple cider vinegar

2 teaspoons sugar

3 eggs

2 tablespoons olive oil

12 ounces ground beef or ground chicken

8 sheets toasted nori or Korean seaweed

### Vegetarian Option

1 (16-oz) package firm tofu

### BULGOGI SAUCE

1 tablespoon soy sauce

1 tablespoon sesame oil

1 tablespoon mirin

1½ teaspoons sugar

½ teaspoon garlic powder

1. **Prep the ingredients** ★★
- **Radishes**—Trim the ends and thinly slice into small strips.
- **Cucumber**—Trim the ends, cut into 2-inch pieces, and thinly slice into small strips.
- **Carrot**—Peel and trim the ends. Cut into 2-inch pieces and thinly slice into small strips.
- **Scallions**—Trim the ends and thinly slice.
- **Bulgogi Sauce**—Combine all the ingredients in a small bowl and mix well.

**Vegetarian option**
- **Tofu**—Drain. Use paper towels to press out the liquid from the tofu. Cut into ½-inch cubes.

2. **Cook the rice** ★★
- Rinse the rice in a colander to remove excess starch.
- In a medium pot, combine the rinsed rice, a pinch of salt, and 3 cups water and bring to a boil over high heat.
- Decrease the heat to low, cover, and simmer for 15 minutes, or until the liquid has been absorbed and the rice is tender.
- Remove from the heat, add 1 tablespoon of soy sauce and 1 tablespoon of sesame oil to the cooked rice, and mix well with a fork.

3. **Make the pickled radishes and carrots (while the rice is cooking)** ★
- In a medium bowl, whisk together 1 tablespoon of rice wine vinegar or apple cider vinegar, 2 teaspoons of sugar, 1 tablespoon water, and ½ teaspoon of salt.
- Add the radish and carrot strips and toss until combined. Let sit for at least 15 minutes.

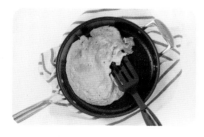

4. **Prep the omelet** ★★
- In a bowl, whisk together the eggs, 1 tablespoon water, and a pinch of salt.
- In a large nonstick skillet, heat 1 tablespoon of olive oil over medium-high heat until hot.
- Add the egg mixture and cook the omelet until the bottom sets and is cooked through, 2 to 3 minutes.
- Carefully flip the omelet onto a cutting board and cut into ½-inch strips.

- **Sauté the meat or tofu** ★★
- In the same skillet, heat the remaining 1 tablespoon of olive oil over medium-high heat until hot.
- Add the ground beef or chicken and, using a fork, crumble the meat and cook until it starts to brown, about 5 minutes.

**Vegetarian option**
- Add the tofu and cook until it starts to brown, 2 to 3 minutes.
- Add the scallions and Bulgogi Sauce and sauté for 2 to 3 minutes.

5. **Assemble and serve the kimbap** ★★
- Place one seaweed sheet on a bamboo mat and spread with a thin layer of rice. Add layers of meat or tofu, sliced cucumber, pickled carrots, pickled radishes, and omelet strips on the lower center of the sheet.
- Lift the bottom of the mat to cover the ingredients. Roll up to the top. Roll with the mat once more to give it a firm shape.
- Repeat with the remaining ingredients. Brush the roll with sesame oil.
- Cut into bite-size pieces.

# Mung Bean Pancakes with Kimchi
## Nokdu Bindaetteok

Made from ground mung beans, nokdu bindaetteok (pronounced nock-due bin-daet-tuhk) is a savory Korean pancake. Sometimes called nok-dujeon, it's a popular street food, and Koreans also cook this classic dish for very special occasions, such as Thanksgiving, Lunar New Year, or birthday parties!

 **SERVES**
4

 **ALLERGENS**
Dairy-Free, Nut-Free, Vegetarian Optional

 **TOTAL PREP & COOK TIME**
45 minutes + 2 days for fermentation

### What You'll Need

2 small turnips or 1 English cucumber

4 scallions

1 tablespoon salt, plus more as needed

3 tablespoons plus ½ teaspoon sugar

3 tablespoons fish sauce or Worcestershire sauce

¾ cup whole mung beans

8 ounces medium shrimp or boneless chicken tenders

½ onion

½ carrot

6 ounces button mushrooms

1 cup all-purpose flour

1 egg

1 cup bean sprouts (optional)

1 tablespoon vegetable oil

3 tablespoons soy sauce

3 tablespoons rice wine vinegar or apple cider vinegar

½ teaspoon sesame seeds (optional)

### Vegetarian Option

Omit the shrimp or chicken

### GARLICKY KIMCHI MIX

1½ tablespoons Korean chili powder

¾ teaspoon garlic powder

¾ teaspoon ground ginger

1. **Make the kimchi
(at least 2 days before serving)** ★★

- **Turnips or cucumber**—Peel and cut into ½-inch cubes.
- **Scallions**—Trim the ends and thinly slice 2 scallions. Cut the remaining 2 scallions into 1½-inch pieces to use in step 3.
- **Garlicky Kimchi Mix**—Combine all the ingredients in a small bowl and mix well.
- In a medium bowl, combine the turnips or cucumber with 1 tablespoon of salt and ½ teaspoon of sugar. Let sit for 45 minutes.
- Rinse the turnips or cucumbers.
- In the same bowl, add the thinly sliced scallions, Garlicky Kimchi Mix, 2 tablespoons of sugar, and 3 tablespoons of fish sauce or Worcestershire sauce and mix until combined.
- Cover and refrigerate for at least 2 days, with the best results if refrigerated for 2 weeks.

2. **Prep the ingredients
(it needs an overnight soak)** ★★

- **Mung beans**—Soak in 3 cups water overnight.
- **Shrimp**—Peel off the shells and remove the tails. Rinse the shrimp and cut them into ¼-inch pieces. OR **Chicken tenders**—Cut into ¼-inch cubes.
- **Onion**—Peel and cut into ¼-inch slices.
- **Carrot**—Peel and shred using a grater.
- **Mushrooms**—Trim the stems and cut into ¼-inch slices.

3. **Prep the pancake batter** ★

- Drain the soaked mung beans, add 1 cup water, and pulse in a blender or food processor for 1 to 2 minutes, or mash them using a potato masher until grainy.
- In a medium bowl, combine the pureed mung beans, shrimp or chicken pieces, flour, onion, remaining scallions, shredded carrot, mushrooms, egg, and bean sprouts (optional) and mix well until combined.
- The batter should be able to coat a spoon. If it is too thick, slowly add water, 1 tablespoon at a time, to reach the desired consistency.

Continued...

# Mung Bean Pancakes with Kimchi
## Nokdu Bindaetteok

### 4. Cook the pancakes ★★

- In a large nonstick skillet or pancake griddle, heat 1 tablespoon of vegetable oil over medium-high heat until hot.
- Pour the batter into the skillet to form 3-inch pancakes about ¾ inch thick.
- Turn down the heat to medium and cook until nicely browned, 3 to 4 minutes. Gently flip the pancakes and cook until nicely browned, 3 to 4 minutes.
- Place the pancakes on a plate and cover with aluminum foil to keep them warm while completing the next batch of pancakes.

### 5. Prep the soy dipping sauce ★

- In a small bowl, whisk together 3 tablespoons of soy sauce, 3 tablespoons of rice wine vinegar or apple cider vinegar, remaining 1 tablespoon of sugar, and ½ teaspoon of sesame seeds (optional) until mixed well.

### 6. Serve your dish ★

- Serve the pancakes with the soy dipping sauce and the turnip or cucumber kimchi.

## DID YOU KNOW...

Jeju Island is home to a unique group of female divers called haenyeo. These skilled divers gather seafood by diving without any breathing apparatus. The longest recorded duration of a haenyeo staying underwater is approximately five minutes!

# Explore Europe

The continent of Europe is the sixth largest in size, out of seven, and the third largest in population. According to the United Nations, there are 44 countries on the continent today. Europe borders the Mediterranean Sea, the Atlantic Ocean, and the continent of Asia.

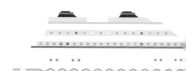

The recipes from six European countries are featured in this section, including:

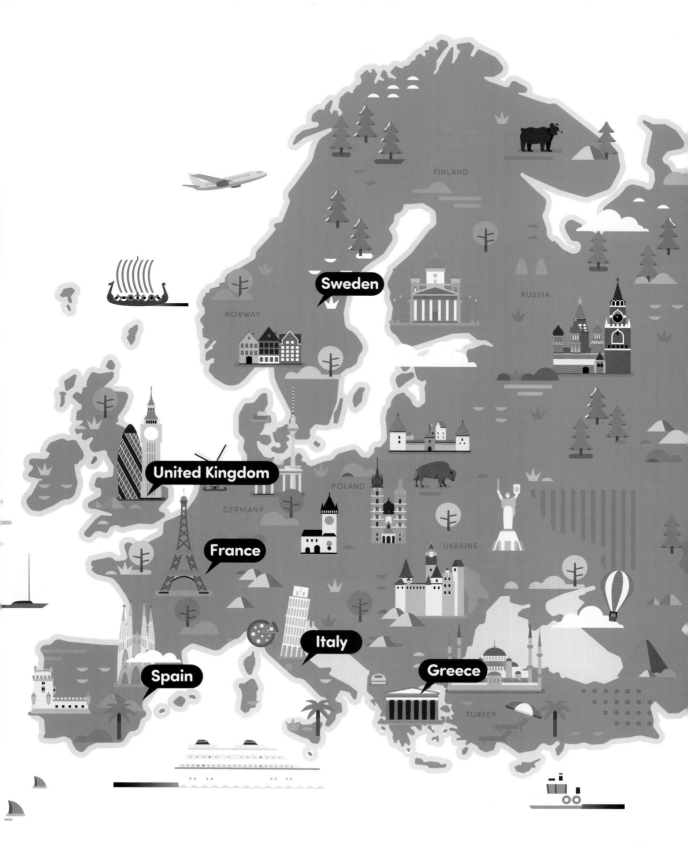

# France

France is the largest country in the European Union and is sometimes called "the hexagon" because of its shape. It borders Belgium to the north, Germany and Switzerland to the east, Spain to the south, and in the west, the English Channel and Bay of Biscay. French culinary practices are revered as the basis of classical cuisine across the Western world. The attention to detail and celebration of individual ingredients have given the French a legendary status among world chefs.

Bon appétit !
(BOHN a-puh-tee)
*"Good appetite!" in French*

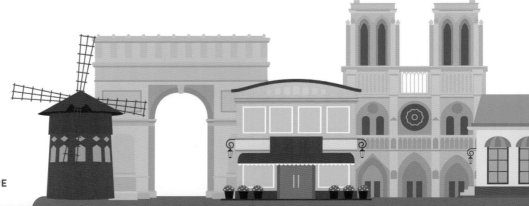

**YOU'LL COOK:**

**Beef Stew with Celery Root Mash (Boeuf Bourguignon)**

**Salmon in Parchment with Tarragon Butter, Squash, and Kale Salad (Saumon en Papillote)**

**Roast Chicken with Vegetables (Poulet Rôti)**

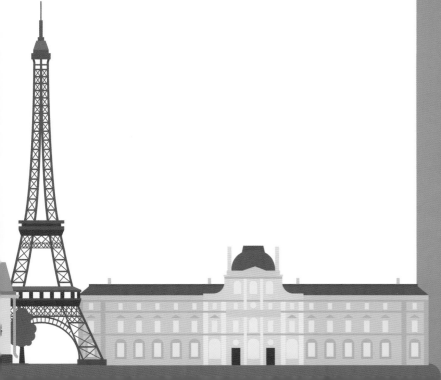

# Beef Stew with Celery Root Mash
## Boeuf Bourguignon

Boeuf bourguignon is so much more than just another beef stew! This classic French dish, made so popular by Julia Child, is the kind of stew you make to impress your family, celebrate a winter birthday, or serve up for the holidays. The deeply savory aroma alone—of onions, slow-cooked beef, and thyme—is appealing to kids and adults alike.

 **SERVES**
4

 **ALLERGENS**
Dairy-Free, Nut-Free

 **TOTAL PREP & COOK TIME**
1½ hours

## What You'll Need

4 ounces bacon

1 large carrot

8 ounces white button mushrooms

1 medium celery root

2 medium potatoes

1½ cups frozen pearl onions or 1 onion

3 sprigs parsley (optional)

2 pounds beef stew cubes (beef chuck recommended)

5 tablespoons all-purpose flour or cornstarch

2 teaspoons salt, plus more as needed

Pepper

1 cup red wine, or ¼ cup apple cider vinegar + ¾ cup water

2 tablespoons butter

½ cup whole milk

French baguette (optional)

## BRAISIN' MIX

¼ cup tomato paste

¼ cup apple cider vinegar

2 tablespoons Worcestershire sauce

1 tablespoon beef or vegetable bouillon

1 teaspoon dried thyme

1 teaspoon dried rosemary

1 teaspoon dried parsley

1 teaspoon garlic powder

1 bay leaf

1. **Prep the ingredients** ★★
- **Bacon**—Cut into ¼-inch slices
- **Carrot**—Peel and dice.
- **Mushrooms**—Rinse and quarter.
- **Celery root**—Peel and dice.
- **Potatoes**—Peel and dice.
- **Onion (if no pearl onions)**—Peel and dice.
- **Parsley (optional)**—Pick off leaves and roughly chop.
- **Braisin' Mix**—Combine all the ingredients in a small bowl and mix well.

2. **Brown the bacon and beef** ★★★
- Season the stew beef cubes with 3 tablespoons of the flour, 1 teaspoon of salt, and pepper to taste. Toss well to coat evenly.
- In a Dutch oven or heavy-bottomed pot with a lid, sauté the bacon over medium-high heat until brown, 2 to 3 minutes. Remove the bacon with a slotted spoon and set aside on a paper towel.
- Add the beef cubes in one layer, without overcrowding (cook in batches, if necessary). Sear until browned, 2 to 3 minutes per side.
- Return all the browned beef back to the pot, add the remaining 2 tablespoons flour or cornstarch, and stir well.

3. **Cook the boeuf bourguignon** ★★★
- Add the bacon, pearl onions or onion, carrots, mushrooms, Braisin' Mix, the wine or vinegar and water mix, 2 cups water, remaining 1 teaspoon of salt, and pepper to taste. Stir well to combine all the ingredients.
- Cover the pot, lower the heat, and simmer for at least 1 hour, adding water if the mixture becomes too dry and stirring occasionally. Taste and season with additional salt and pepper. Remove the bay leaf.
- Note: If preparing in advance, stop here and let the stew cool to room temperature. Cover and refrigerate until ready for reheating at a later stage.

4. **Make the celery root mash (while the beef stew is braising)** ★★
- In a large pot filled with salted water, add the celery root and potatoes, making sure at least 1 inch of water covers the vegetables. Bring to a boil over high heat and cook until tender, 8 to 10 minutes.
- Drain in a colander and return to the pot. Add 2 tablespoons of butter and ½ cup of whole milk. Mash until smooth, adding more milk if necessary. Add salt and pepper to taste.
- Cover the pot and reheat briefly before serving.

5. **Serve your dish** ★
- Divide the celery root and potato mash among individual bowls. Spoon the boeuf bourguignon over the mash, sprinkle with chopped parsley (optional), and serve.
- **Optional**—Serve with a sliced French baguette to soak up some of the yummy sauce!

# Salmon in Parchment with Tarragon Butter, Squash, and Kale Salad
## Saumon en Papillote

En papillote (on poppy-YOTE) is a French method of slow-cooking fish in parchment paper packets. The sealed paper parcel retains moisture and steams the food. Fish is delicate and cooks quickly, which is why en papillote is an ideal (and almost odorless) way to cook it!

**SERVES**
4

**ALLERGENS**
Dairy-Free, Nut-Free, Gluten-Free

**TOTAL PREP & COOK TIME**
55 minutes

### What You'll Need

1 pound (about 3) delicata squash or sweet potatoes

1 Fuji or Gala apple

1 lemon

2 shallots or 1 small onion

5 sprigs tarragon

3 tablespoons butter

3 tablespoons olive oil

1½ teaspoons salt, plus more as needed

1 teaspoon pepper, plus more as needed

2 teaspoons honey or maple syrup (optional)

Parchment paper

4 (6-oz) salmon, cod, or snapper fillets

6 ounces baby kale

### TARRA HERBIE MIX

2 teaspoons garlic powder

1½ teaspoons dried tarragon

1 teaspoon chicken or vegetable bouillon

½ teaspoon lemon peel granules

### ÉPICES DÉLICATE

1 teaspoon chili powder

1 teaspoon ground cinnamon

1 teaspoon sugar

  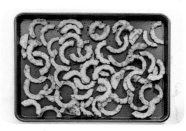

1. **Prep the ingredients** ★★
- Preheat the oven to 425°F.
- **Delicata squash**—Trim the ends and cut in half lengthwise. Using a spoon, remove the seeds and cut into ½-inch slices. OR **Sweet potatoes**—Peel and cut into 1-inch cubes.
- **Apple**—Cut in half, remove the core, and cut into ½-inch slices.
- **Lemon**—Cut in half. Juice half the lemon for step 5. Cut the remaining half into wedges for step 6.
- **Shallots or onion**—Peel and dice. Use half for step 2 and half for step 5.
- **Tarragon**—Pick off the leaves and finely chop.
- **Tarra Herbie Mix**—Combine all the ingredients in a small bowl and mix well.
- **Épices Délicate**—Combine all the ingredients in a small bowl and mix well.

2. **Make the tarragon butter** ★
- In a small bowl, cut 3 tablespoons of butter into ½-inch cubes.
- Add the chopped tarragon, Tarra Herbie Mix, and half the shallots or onion.
- Using a fork, mash the ingredients together until evenly mixed.

3. **Roast the delicata squash or sweet potatoes** ★★★
- On a baking sheet, combine the delicata squash or sweet potatoes, Épices Délicate, 1 tablespoon of olive oil, 1 teaspoon of salt, 1 teaspoon of pepper, and 1 teaspoon of honey or maple syrup (optional). Toss well to coat the vegetables.
- Spread out the squash or potatoes evenly in a single layer.
- Bake until tender, 25 to 30 minutes.

Continued...

# Salmon in Parchment with Tarragon Butter, Squash, and Kale Salad
## Saumon en Papillote

**4. Make the fish en papillotes** ⭐⭐
**(while the squash is roasting)**

- Cut 4 pieces of parchment paper, each at least 16 inches long (one for each fillet). Place a fish fillet in the middle of a sheet of parchment paper. Season lightly with salt and pepper.
- Divide the tarragon butter evenly over each fillet.
- Fold the paper over fillet by overlapping the paper, twisting the excess paper at the ends, and folding it under the packet to seal the ingredients inside. Repeat with the rest of the fillets.
- Place the packets on a baking sheet, lower the oven temperature to 350°F, and bake until cooked through, about 10 minutes or longer, depending on the thickness of the fillets.

**5. Make the kale salad** ⭐
**(while the fish and squash are baking)**

- In a large bowl, whisk together 1 tablespoon of lemon juice, remaining 2 tablespoons of olive oil, remaining 1 teaspoon of honey or maple syrup, remaining ½ teaspoon of salt, and pepper to taste.
- Add the remaining shallots or onion, the apple, and the baby kale and toss well to combine.

**6. Serve your dish** ⭐

- Divide the squash or sweet potatoes among individual plates. Place one fish packet on each plate and carefully cut it open with scissors or a knife.
- Serve with the kale salad and squeeze the lemon wedges over the fish to further enhance the taste.

## DID YOU KNOW...

France is known for its love of baguettes. It is estimated that around 10 billion baguettes are consumed in France each year! The traditional baguette has strict regulations regarding its ingredients and baking process.

# Roast Chicken with Vegetables
## Poulet Rôti

Pronounced "POO-lay ROH-tee," this roast chicken is easy to make, but the real secret to the famously tasty French dish is how the chickens are fed and raised. The birds in France roam freely, happily pecking and scratching in the grass, and their foraged food is supplemented with milk and corn. To get the most authentic flavor, if possible, use free-range chicken to duplicate this beloved recipe.

 **SERVES**
4

 **ALLERGENS**
Dairy-Free, Nut-Free, Gluten-Free

 **TOTAL PREP & COOK TIME**
1 hour 20 minutes + 2 hours chilling time for optional crispy skin

### What You'll Need

1 (3½- to 4-lb) free-range whole chicken

4 teaspoons salt, plus more as needed

1 teaspoon pepper, plus more as needed

1 lemon

1 large onion

3 garlic cloves

1 large carrot

3 medium potatoes

3 medium beets

2 tablespoons butter

1 tablespoon olive oil

### ZESTY PROVENCE MIX

1 tablespoon dried rosemary

1 tablespoon dried thyme

1½ teaspoons garlic powder

½ teaspoon lemon peel granules

1 bay leaf

### OO-LA-LA! GRAVY MIX

1 tablespoon cornstarch

2 teaspoons chicken bouillon

½ teaspoon lemon peel granules

1. **Prep the ingredients** ★★
- Preheat the oven to 425°F.
- **Chicken**—Remove the giblet and other internal organs from the chicken cavity. Rinse and pat the chicken completely dry with paper towels. Season generously with 3 teaspoons of salt and pepper to taste. (Optional—For crispier skin, leave the chicken uncovered in the fridge for at least 2 hours.)
- **Lemon**—Cut into quarters.
- **Onion**—Peel and thinly slice.
- **Garlic**—Peel and leave whole.
- **Carrot**—Peel and dice.
- **Potatoes**—Peel and cut into 1½-inch cubes.
- **Beets**—Peel and cut into 1½-inch cubes.
- **Zesty Provence Mix**—Combine all the ingredients in a small bowl and mix well.
- **Oo-la-la! Gravy Mix**—Combine all the ingredients in a small bowl and mix well.

2. **Prep and roast the chicken** ★★★
- Place the garlic cloves and 2 lemon quarters in the chicken cavity and rub the chicken all over with 2 tablespoons of the Zesty Provence Mix.
- In a Dutch oven or large ovenproof pot, heat 2 tablespoons of butter over medium-high heat. Add the chicken and brown on all sides, 5 to 6 minutes per side.
- Scatter the onion and carrots around the chicken and cover the pot tightly to retain the moisture as it roasts. Place the pot in the oven and roast until the chicken is cooked through, about 1 hour. (Note: A thermometer should register 160°F in the thickest part of breast and 175°F in the thigh.)

3. **Roast the vegetables (at the same time as the chicken)** ★★★
- On a baking sheet, combine the potatoes, beets, remaining Zesty Provence Mix, 1 tablespoon of olive oil, the remaining 1 teaspoon of salt, and 1 teaspoon of pepper. Toss well to coat.
- Spread the vegetables out evenly on the baking sheet. Place the baking sheet in the oven (along with the chicken in the pot) and roast until the vegetables begin to soften, 15 to 20 minutes.
- Remove the baking sheet from the oven, remove the bay leaf, and cover with aluminum foil to keep warm while the chicken finishes roasting.

Continued...

# Roast Chicken with Vegetables
## Poulet Rôti

**4. Prep the chicken jus**

- When chicken is done, transfer the chicken to a carving board, cover with foil, and let rest while you prepare the jus.
- In a bowl, whisk together the Oo-la-la! Gravy Mix and 1½ cups water. Add the gravy mixture to the pot the chicken was just in and stir over medium-high heat until the sauce thickens. Add water until the sauce reaches the desired consistency. Cook until heated through and add salt and pepper to taste.
- Strain the jus into a bowl for serving.

**5. Serve your dish**

- Carve the chicken into pieces, place them on a platter, and serve with the chicken jus and roasted vegetables on the side.

## DID YOU KNOW...

France is home to 45 UNESCO World Heritage Sites, ranging from architectural marvels like Mont-Saint-Michel and Chartres Cathedral to natural wonders like the Mont Perdu and the Gulf of Porto.

# Greece

As one of the oldest European civilizations, Greece has local traditions of food and culture dating back 4,000 years. Ancient roots and herbs play a big role in Greek cuisine, where herbs like oregano, mint, garlic, onion, dill, bay leaves, basil, thyme, and fennel seed are all considered key seasonings in Greek food.

Καλή όρεξη
kali orexi
(kah-LEE oh-REH-ksee)
*"Enjoy your meal!" in Greek*

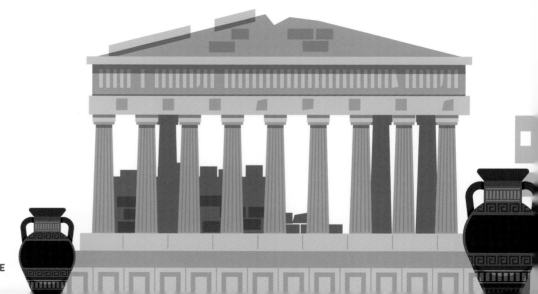

**YOU'LL COOK:**

**Chicken or Pork or Vegetarian Skewers with Cucumber Yogurt Sauce and Pita Pockets (Souvláki me Tzatzíki)**

**Greek Lamb or Vegetable Burgers with Tomato and Cucumber Salad (Biftékia)**

**Greek Baked Cod or Cauliflower Steaks with Roasted Vegetables (Psari Plaki)**

# Chicken or Pork or Vegetarian Skewers with Cucumber Yogurt Sauce and Pita Pockets
## Souvlaki me Tzatziki

"Souvlaki" is the Greek name for meat grilled on a skewer, their version of fast food. Cubes of chicken breast are marinated, then skewered and broiled until golden brown. Bursting with flavor, souvlaki is then tucked inside warm pita pockets and topped with a cucumber tzatziki sauce, lettuce, and tomatoes. Get creative with your own version—veggies, steak, or seafood will all taste great!

 **SERVES**
4

 **ALLERGENS**
Nut-Free, Gluten-Free Optional, Vegetarian Optional

 **TOTAL PREP & COOK TIME**
30 minutes

### What You'll Need

8 wooden skewers

2 small cucumbers

1 beefsteak tomato

2 pounds boneless skinless chicken breast or thighs or pork tenderloin

1 lemon (optional)

2 tablespoons red wine vinegar

3 tablespoons olive oil

2½ teaspoons salt

1 teaspoon sugar

Pepper

½ cup plain Greek yogurt or plant-based yogurt

4 pita pockets or gluten-free pita pockets

4 leaves Boston lettuce

### Vegetarian Option

2 zucchini

1 red bell pepper

1 red onion

### GROOVY SOUVY MIX

1½ teaspoons dried oregano

1 teaspoon sugar

1 teaspoon dried dill

1 teaspoon garlic powder

¼ teaspoon lemon peel granules

¼ teaspoon onion powder

### T'ZIKI MIX

1 teaspoon dried dill

1 teaspoon garlic powder

¼ teaspoon lemon peel granules

### 1. Prep the ingredients ★★

- **Skewers**—Soak in water for at least 10 minutes.
- **Cucumbers**—Trim the ends and grate.
- **Tomato**—Thinly slice.
- **Pork or Chicken**—Cut into 1½-inch cubes.
- **(Optional) Lemon**—Using a grater or zester, grate 1 teaspoon of lemon zest. Save the rest of the lemon for another use.
- **Groovy Souvy Mix**—Combine all the ingredients in a small bowl and mix well.
- **T'ziki Mix**—Combine all the ingredients in a small bowl and mix well.

**Vegetarian option**

- **Zucchini**—Trim the ends and cut to 1½-inch pieces.
- **Bell pepper**—Remove the stem and seeds and cut into 1½-inch pieces.
- **Onion**—Peel and cut into 1½-inch pieces.

### 2. Prep and broil the souvlaki ★★★

- In a medium bowl, combine the meat or vegetables, Groovy Souvy Mix, 2 tablespoons of red wine vinegar, 2 tablespoons of olive oil, 2 teaspoons of salt, 1 teaspoon of sugar, and pepper to taste. Toss to coat evenly and let marinate for at least 10 minutes.
- Adjust the top oven rack to 6 inches below the broiler. Preheat the broiler to high.
- Thread the meat or vegetables onto the skewers and place them on a baking sheet.
- Broil for about 8 minutes, flipping the skewers carefully halfway through.

### 3. Make the tzatziki ★

- In a medium bowl, whisk together ½ cup of Greek yogurt, T'ziki Mix, 1 teaspoon of lemon zest (optional), remaining 1 tablespoon of olive oil, remaining ½ teaspoon of salt, and pepper to taste.
- Wrap the cucumber in a paper towel and twist it tightly over a bowl to remove the liquid.
- Add the cucumber to the Greek yogurt mix and stir to combine.

### 4. Warm the pita pockets ★

- Microwave the pita pockets or gluten-free pita pockets until pliable, about 1 minute.

### 5. Serve your dish ★

- Carefully remove the meat or vegetables from the skewers and place them in a pita pocket.
- Top with lettuce, tomato, and tzatziki sauce.

# Greek Lamb or Vegetable Burgers with Tomato and Cucumber Salad
## Biftékia

These scrumptious burgers taste like the Mediterranean! Enveloped by a warm pita pocket, topped with a Greek yogurt sauce, and served with tomato and cucumber salad, our lamb burgers will transport you to Greece! They are great cooked on the grill in the summer, but you can sauté them in a skillet year-round and get those sunny flavors whenever you like.

**SERVES**
4

**ALLERGENS**
Nut-Free, Gluten-Free Optional, Vegetarian Optional

**TOTAL PREP & COOK TIME**
25 minutes

### What You'll Need

1 cup cherry tomatoes

1 large cucumber or 5 small cucumbers

1 lemon

4 tablespoons olive oil

2 teaspoons salt, plus more as needed

1½ pounds ground lamb

½ cup plain Greek yogurt or plant-based yogurt

2 pita breads or gluten-free pita breads

### Vegetarian Option

2 (15-oz) cans black beans

1 cup breadcrumbs

1 egg

### SAVORY MEDITI-O! MIX

1 tablespoon dried oregano

2 teaspoons ground coriander

2 teaspoons ground cumin

2 teaspoons garlic powder

### HERBIE MEDITI-O! MIX

1 teaspoon dried oregano

1 teaspoon garlic powder

¼ teaspoon lemon peel granules

### 1. Prep the ingredients ★★

- **Cherry tomatoes**—Cut in half.
- **Cucumber**—Trim the ends and cut into ⅛-inch slices.
- **Lemon**—Cut in half and juice. Use in step 2 and 4.
- **Savory Mediti-o! Mix**—Combine all the ingredients in a small bowl and mix well.
- **Herbie Mediti-o! Mix**—Combine all the ingredients in a small bowl and mix well.

### 2. Assemble the salad ★

- In a medium bowl, whisk together 2 tablespoons of olive oil, 2 teaspoons of lemon juice, 1 teaspoon of the Herbie Mediti-o! Mix, and ½ teaspoon of salt. Add the cucumbers and tomatoes and toss well to combine. Refrigerate the salad.

### 3. Make and cook the burgers ★★★

- In a large bowl, combine the ground lamb, Savory Mediti-o! Mix, and 1 teaspoon of salt.

**Vegetarian option**

- In a large bowl, combine the black beans, Savory Mediti-o! Mix, breadcrumbs, egg, and 1 teaspoon of salt. Mash with a fork until the mixture is well combined.
- Form the meat or vegetable mixture into 4 patties.
- In a large skillet, heat 1 tablespoon of olive oil over medium-high heat until hot.
- Add the patties and cook through, 3 to 4 minutes per side.

### 4. Prep the yogurt sauce and warm the pita ★

- In a small bowl, combine the remaining 1 tablespoon of olive oil, Greek yogurt, remaining Herbie Mediti-o! Mix, 1 teaspoon of lemon juice, remaining ½ teaspoon of salt, and pepper to taste and mix.
- Cut the pita breads in half and warm in a microwave oven until pliable, 15 to 30 seconds.

### 5. Serve your dish ★

- Place each lamb burger or veggie burger in a warm pita pocket.
- Top with the Greek yogurt sauce and serve with the tomato and cucumber salad.

# Greek Baked Cod or Cauliflower Steaks with Roasted Vegetables
## Psari Plaki

Greece is composed of almost 6,000 islands in the Mediterranean, so naturally seafood is central to its cuisine! Psari plaki (sah-ree PLAH-kee) is a traditional Greek fish dish, and this recipe uses cod. The fillets are baked with spiced potatoes, onions, and fennel until meltingly tender. Topped with lemon slices, this light and flavorful dish is as beautiful as it is delicious.

 **SERVES**
4

 **ALLERGENS**
Dairy-Free, Nut-Free, Gluten-Free, Vegetarian Optional

 **TOTAL PREP & COOK TIME**
40 minutes

### What You'll Need

1 lemon

1 large onion

1 fennel bulb

3 Yukon Gold potatoes (about 1½ pounds)

2 tablespoons olive oil

2½ teaspoons salt

Pepper

4 (6-oz) cod fillets

### Vegetarian Option

2 heads cauliflower

### ROOT VEGGIE MIX

2 teaspoons dried oregano

1½ teaspoons dried thyme

1 teaspoon fennel seeds

¼ teaspoon lemon peel granules

### TARRA HERBIE MIX

2 teaspoons garlic powder

1½ teaspoons dried tarragon

1 teaspoon chicken or vegetable bouillon

½ teaspoon lemon peel granules

### 1. Prep the ingredients ⭐⭐

- Preheat the oven to 425°F.
- **Lemon**—Grate the zest to be used in step 2. Then thinly slice the lemon into rounds and remove the seeds, to be used in step 3.
- **Onion**—Peel and thinly slice.
- **Fennel**—Fronds: Roughly chop for step 4. Bulb: Cut in half. Discard the core and tough outer layer, then thinly slice into rings for step 2.
- **Potatoes**—Peel and cut into 1½-inch cubes.
- **Root Veggie Mix**—In a bowl, combine all the ingredients in a small bowl and mix well.
- **Tarra Herbie Mix**—In a bowl, combine all the ingredients in a small bowl and mix well.

**Vegetarian option**

- **Cauliflower**—Cut the heads vertically into 1½-inch slices (you should have at least 6). Note: Don't worry if you end up with florets—they'll still be delicious!

### 2. Roast the vegetables ⭐⭐⭐

- In a large bowl, toss the onion, fennel, and potatoes with the lemon zest, Root Veggie Mix, 2 tablespoons of olive oil, 1½ teaspoons of salt, and pepper to taste.
- Spread the mixture in a baking dish.
- Cover with aluminum foil and roast until the vegetables are softened, about 15 minutes.

### 3. Bake the fish ⭐⭐⭐

- Sprinkle the fish fillets or cauliflower steaks with the Tarra Herbie Mix, remaining 1 teaspoon of salt, and pepper to taste.
- Remove the foil from the baking dish and lightly toss the vegetables.
- Place the fish fillets or cauliflower steaks on top of the vegetables and place the lemon rounds over the fish or cauliflower. Cover with the foil again and bake until cooked through, 12 to 15 minutes.

### 4. Serve your dish ⭐

- Place the fish or cauliflower steak topped with lemon slices on individual plates along with the roasted vegetables.
- Spoon the pan juices over the fish or cauliflower steak. Top with some of the fennel fronds.

# Italy

Italy surrounds two of the world's smallest countries—San Marino in Northern Italy, which is the oldest republic in the world, and Vatican City in Rome, the smallest country in the world. The country is surrounded on three sides by water: the Tyrrhenian Sea to the west, the Adriatic Sea to the east, and the Ionian Sea to the south, which are all part of the Mediterranean Sea.

As cookbook author Marcella Hazan said, "Italian food is twice blessed, because it is the product of two arts—the art of cooking and the art of eating." Family plays a central role in Italian traditions, and a large family meal is still customary in many Italian households.

Buon appetito!
(BWAN ah-pah-TEE-to)
*"Enjoy your meal!" in Italian*

**YOU'LL COOK:**

**Meatballs and Spaghetti with Caesar Salad (Polpette di Spaghetti)**

**Breaded and Fried Chicken or Tofu with Vegetables and Arugula Salad (Cotoletta alla Milenese)**

**Escarole and White Bean Soup with Garlic Bread (Zuppa di Scarola e Fagioli)**

**DID YOU KNOW...**

- Italy has more than 55 UNESCO World Heritage Sites, more than any other country.

- All three of Europe's active volcanoes are in Italy—Etna, Vesuvius, and Stromboli.

- The Colosseum in Rome is an ancient amphitheater and one of the most iconic landmarks in Italy. Built in the 1st century AD, it could hold up to 50,000 spectators and was used for gladiatorial contests, animal hunts, and other public spectacles.

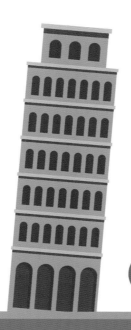

# Meatballs and Spaghetti with Caesar Salad
## Polpette di Spaghetti

In Italy, meatballs are very popular and are usually served as a starter. Our recipe broils the meatballs instead of frying them, which makes them much tidier to cook, healthier to eat, and easier to prepare on a busy weeknight. We've paired the meatballs with spaghetti and marinara, a style originated by Italian immigrants in the United States, though it is unlikely to be served that way in Italy.

**SERVES**
4

**ALLERGENS**
Nut-Free, Gluten-Free Optional, Vegetarian Optional

**TOTAL PREP & COOK TIME**
50 minutes

### What You'll Need

4 tablespoons olive oil, plus more as needed

1 head romaine lettuce

1 lemon

2 (15-oz) cans tomato puree

2¼ teaspoons salt, plus more as needed

1 teaspoon sugar

1½ pounds ground beef or chicken

1 cup panko, breadcrumbs, or gluten-free panko

1 large egg

½ cup milk or cream

1 cup plus 1 tablespoon grated Parmesan cheese, plus more for garnish

Pepper

8 ounces spaghetti or gluten-free spaghetti

2 tablespoons mayonnaise (optional)

### Vegetarian Option

6 ounces mushrooms

1 (16-oz) package extra-firm tofu or 12 ounces plant-based "meat"

### HERBIE HERB MIX

2 teaspoons dried oregano

2 teaspoons dried basil

2 teaspoons dried thyme

2 teaspoons granulated garlic

¼ teaspoon red pepper flakes

### CAESAR DRESSING

2 tablespoons Worcestershire sauce

1 teaspoon Dijon mustard

### 1. Prep the ingredients ★★

- Lightly grease a baking sheet with olive oil.
- **Romaine lettuce**—Separate the leaves, rinse, and pat or spin dry. Cut into bite-size pieces.
- **Lemon**—Cut in half and juice. Use 1 tablespoon in step 6, and save the rest for another use.
- **Herbie Herb Mix**—Combine all the ingredients in a bowl and mix well.
- **Caesar Dressing**—Combine all the ingredients in a bowl and mix well.

**Vegetarian option**

- **Mushrooms**—Rinse and mince.
- **Tofu**—Drain. Use paper towels to press out the liquid from the tofu. Crumble into small pieces.

### 2. Make the marinara sauce ★★

- In a Dutch oven or large pot, heat 1 tablespoon of olive oil over medium-high heat.
- Add the tomato puree, 3 tablespoons of the Herbie Herb Mix, 1 teaspoon of salt, and 1 teaspoon of sugar and stir well.
- Bring to a boil and let simmer while preparing the meatballs.

### 3. Form the meatballs (while the sauce is cooking) ★

- In a large bowl, combine the ground meat or mushrooms and tofu or plant-based "meat," panko or breadcrumbs, remaining Herbie Herb Mix, egg, ½ cup of milk or cream, 1 cup of Parmesan cheese, 1 teaspoon of salt, and pepper to taste and gently mix until combined.
- Form the mixture into meatballs about 1½ inches in diameter (you can use a small ice cream scoop!).
- Place on the prepared baking sheet.

### 4. Broil and cook the meatballs in sauce ★★★

- Adjust the top oven rack to 6 inches below the broiler. Preheat the broiler to high.
- Broil the meatballs until golden brown and cooked through, 8 to 10 minutes. Be sure to keep an eye on them the entire time so they don't burn!
- Remove the meatballs from the oven and carefully add them to the simmering marinara sauce. Continue to simmer the sauce while you prepare the pasta.

### 5. Cook the pasta (while the meatballs simmer) ★★

- Bring a large pot of salted water to a boil.
- Once boiling, add the pasta and cook until al dente (firm to the bite but not overcooked), 8 to 10 minutes. Drain the pasta in a colander.
- In a large bowl, combine the pasta with the meatballs and marinara sauce and toss until evenly coated.
- Cover the bowl to keep warm while you prepare the Caesar salad.

### 6. Make the Caesar salad and serve your dish ★

- In a medium bowl, whisk together the Caesar Dressing mix, remaining 1 tablespoon of Parmesan cheese, 1 tablespoon of lemon juice, 2 tablespoons of mayonnaise (optional), remaining 3 tablespoons of olive oil, remaining ¼ teaspoon of salt, and pepper to taste until emulsified.
- Add the chopped lettuce and toss until well coated. Place a large serving of meatballs and spaghetti on individual plates and top with additional grated Parmesan. Serve with the Caesar salad.

# Breaded and Fried Chicken or Tofu with Vegetables and Arugula Salad
## Cotoletta alla Milenese

A signature dish from Milan, this recipe is made with thin slices of meat, which are breaded and cooked, an easy and delicious preparation. This technique was first described in a document from 1148, and it is still preserved in the Basilica of Saint Ambrose. Kids will have fun dipping the meat in bowls of flour, egg wash, and breadcrumbs before cooking them in a skillet.

**SERVES**
4

**ALLERGENS**
Nut-Free,
Vegetarian Optional

**TOTAL PREP & COOK TIME**
50 minutes

## What You'll Need

1 pound sweet potatoes

1 pound Yukon Gold potatoes

1 red onion

1 shallot

1 lemon

4 tablespoons olive oil

3 teaspoons salt

Pepper

1 cup all-purpose flour

2 large eggs

1 cup panko, breadcrumbs, or gluten-free panko

2 pounds thinly sliced chicken or veal cutlets

5 ounces baby arugula

## Vegetarian Option

2 (16-oz) packages extra-firm tofu

## ROSIE MIX

1 teaspoon dried rosemary

1 teaspoon granulated garlic

½ teaspoon lemon peel granules

## BALSAMY VINNY MIX

1½ tablespoons balsamic vinegar

1 teaspoon honey

### 1. Prep the ingredients ★★

- Preheat the oven to 425°F.
- **Sweet potatoes**—Peel and cut into 1-inch cubes.
- **Potatoes**—Peel and cut into 1-inch cubes.
- **Red onion**—Peel and cut into 1-inch pieces.
- **Shallot**—Peel and mince.
- **Lemon**—Cut into wedges.
- **Rosie Mix**—Combine all the ingredients in a small bowl and mix well.
- **Balsamy Vinny Mix**—Combine all the ingredients in a small bowl and mix well.

**Vegetarian option**

- **Tofu**—Drain. Use paper towels to press out the liquid from the tofu. Cut into ½-inch slices.

### 2. Roast the vegetables ★★

- On a baking sheet, combine the sweet potatoes, potatoes, red onion, 1½ teaspoons of the Rosie Mix, 1 tablespoon of olive oil, 1 teaspoon of salt, and pepper to taste.
- Toss well and evenly spread the vegetables on the baking sheet. Roast for 10 to 12 minutes. Flip the vegetables and roast until golden brown and cooked through, 10 to 12 minutes more.

### 3. Bread the chicken ★

- Set up a breading station in this order: Bowl 1: flour; bowl 2: whisk the egg with 2 teaspoons water; bowl 3: panko or breadcrumbs and remaining Rosie Mix and mix well.
- Pat the chicken or veal cutlets or tofu steak dry with paper towels and season with 1 teaspoon of salt and pepper to taste.
- Using clean hands, dip each piece of chicken of tofu into the flour in bowl 1 until completely covered. Dip the piece into the egg in bowl 2, dripping off any excess back into the bowl, and finally dip the piece into the breadcrumbs in bowl 3.
- Place each breaded piece of chicken or tofu on a plate or baking sheet.

### 4. Cook the chicken or tofu ★★★

- Heat 1 tablespoon of oil in a large cast-iron or nonstick skillet until hot.
- Add the breaded meat or tofu in one layer and cook until golden brown, 3 to 4 minutes per side. Cook in batches and add oil if the pan begins to look dry.
- Place the cooked meat or tofu on a plate and keep warm until ready to serve.

### 5. Make the salad ★

- In a large bowl, whisk together the Balsamy Vinny Mix, minced shallot, remaining 2 tablespoons of olive oil, remaining 1 teaspoon of salt, and pepper to taste.
- Add the arugula and toss until evenly coated.

### 6. Serve your dish ★

- Place roasted root vegetables on individual plates along with a piece of meat or tofu and some of the arugula salad.
- Serve with lemon wedges on the side to squeeze over the Milanese.

# Escarole and White Bean Soup with Garlic Bread
## Zuppa di Scarola e Fagioli

This soup is a traditional dish from the Campania region in Southern Italy and is ideal for warming up cold winter evenings. It is considered a one-pot peasant dish—one that is easy to make, delicious, nutritious, and affordable! If you have a leftover Parmesan cheese rind in the fridge, add it to the soup to give it a creamier and cheesier flavor.

 **SERVES**
4

 **ALLERGENS**
Dairy-Free, Nut-Free, Gluten-Free Optional, Vegetarian

 **TOTAL PREP & COOK TIME**
20 minutes

## WHAT YOU'LL NEED

1 large bunch escarole

1 leek

1 carrot

3 garlic cloves

1 lemon

2 (14.5-oz) cans cannellini beans

1 tablespoon olive oil

1½ teaspoons salt

Pepper

¼ teaspoon red pepper flakes (optional)

1 piece Parmesan cheese rind (optional)

1 baguette or gluten-free bread

4 tablespoons butter

2 ounces grated Parmesan cheese

## SOUPIE MIX

4½ teaspoons vegetable bouillon

¼ teaspoon dried thyme

1 bay leaf

### 1. Prep the ingredients ★★

- Preheat the oven to 400°F.
- **Escarole**—Remove and discard the stems. Rinse the leaves and roughly chop into 1-inch pieces.
- **Leek**—Trim the root and green part, cut in half lengthwise, thinly slice, and place them in a bowl of water. Use your hands to break up the leek slices to remove the dirt. Lift the leeks from the water without disturbing the dirt that has settled on the bottom.
- **Carrot**—Peel and trim the ends. Cut into small cubes.
- **Garlic**—Peel and mince or crush with a garlic press. Use half in step 2 and half in step 3.
- **Lemon**—Cut into 4 wedges.
- **Cannellini beans**—Drain and rinse in a colander.
- **Soupie Mix**—Combine all the ingredients in a bowl and mix well.

### 2. Prep the soup ★★

- In a Dutch oven or large pot, heat 1 tablespoon of olive oil over medium-high heat until hot.
- Add the leek and sauté until softened, 1 to 2 minutes. Add the carrot, half the minced garlic, 1½ teaspoons salt, and pepper to taste and sauté for 2 to 3 minutes.
- Add the Soupie Mix, escarole, cannellini beans, 4 cups water, red pepper flakes (optional), and Parmesan rind (optional).
- Bring to a boil and simmer for 15 minutes.

### 3. Make the garlic bread ★★

- **Baguette**—Cut in half lengthwise.
- Combine 4 tablespoons of butter and the remaining minced garlic in a microwave-safe bowl and microwave until the butter is melted.
- Using a pastry brush, spread the garlic butter on the cut side of the bread halves.
- Sprinkle with three-quarters of the grated Parmesan. Put the halves together like a sandwich, tightly wrap the bread in aluminum foil, and bake for 10 minutes.
- Remove from the oven and keep the bread wrapped in foil until ready to serve.

### 4. Serve your dish ★

- Stir the soup. Using a potato masher, mash some of the beans in the pot to thicken the soup.
- Ladle the warm soup into bowls. Squeeze some lemon juice over each bowl to brighten up the flavors and garnish with the remaining grated Parmesan cheese.
- Cut the garlic bread into slices and serve alongside for dipping.

# Spain

This country is the third largest in Europe. Traditional Spanish dishes use local ingredients, which are very different from region to region within the country, making for diverse and exciting down-to-earth recipes that have been made traditionally for hundreds of years.

¡Buen provecho!
(buen pro-BE-cho)
*"Enjoy your meal!" in Spanish*

## YOU'LL COOK:

**Chicken or Vegetable Rice with Tomato and Peas (Paella)**

**Garlicky Shrimp or Mushrooms and Toast with Tomato (Gambas al Ajillo y Pan con Tomate)**

**Spanish Omelet with Onion and Bell Pepper (Tortilla Española)**

## DID YOU KNOW...

- Spanish is the world's second-most spoken language, second to Mandarin (China).

- Spain has the oldest restaurant in the world— El Restaurante Botín in Madrid opened in 1725.

- Around 44 percent of the world's olive oil is produced by Spain.

# Chicken or Vegetable Rice with Tomato and Peas
## Paella

This Valencian all-in-one rice dish is from the eastern coast of Spain. In our version, we simmer chicken thighs and drumsticks in rice, vegetables, spices, and chicken broth, creating a balanced and flavorful weekday dinner. A short-grain rice like Arborio is just right for this dish. Saffron gives it a rich, golden color and a unique aroma to make an impressive-looking meal that will wow the family!

**SERVES**
4

**ALLERGENS**
Nut-Free, Gluten-Free, Vegetarian Optional

**TOTAL PREP & COOK TIME**
1 hour

### What You'll Need

1 large onion

2 red bell peppers

½ cup pitted green olives (optional)

4 chicken drumsticks and 4 thighs

1 teaspoon salt

1 teaspoon pepper

2 tablespoons olive oil

1 (15-oz) can diced tomatoes

2 cups Arborio rice

1 cup frozen baby peas

### Vegetarian Option

1 (14-oz) can artichoke hearts

8 ounces asparagus or green beans

### PAPPI' PAELLA SPICE

1 tablespoon dried oregano

2 teaspoons ground cumin

2 teaspoons vegetable or chicken bouillon

1 teaspoon garlic powder

¼ teaspoon crushed saffron threads

2 bay leaves

### 1. Prep the ingredients

- Preheat the oven to 375°F.
- **Onion**—Peel and dice.
- **Red bell peppers**—Cut in half, discard the stem and seeds, and dice.
- **Green olives (optional)**—Roughly chop.
- **Pappi' Paella Spice**—Combine all the ingredients in a small bowl and mix well.

**Vegetarian option**

- **Artichoke hearts**—Drain and cut into quarters.
- **Asparagus or green beans**—Trim off the ends and cut into 1-inch pieces.

### 2. Brown the chicken

- Season the chicken with 1 teaspoon of salt and 1 teaspoon of pepper.
- In a Dutch oven or ovenproof pan with a lid, heat 1 tablespoon of olive oil over medium-high heat until hot. Without crowding the pan, add the chicken and cook until golden brown on both sides, about 6 minutes. Transfer the chicken to a plate. Repeat with the remaining chicken. Set aside on a plate.

### 3. Sauté the vegetables

- In the same pan, heat the remaining 1 tablespoon of olive oil over medium-high heat until hot.
- Add the onion, red bell peppers, diced tomatoes, and Pappi' Paella Spice mix. Sauté until the vegetables are tender, about 5 minutes.

### 4. Prep and bake the paella

- Add the rice to the same pan, stirring to coat all the grains.
- Add 2 cups water and stir well to mix. Add the chicken and any juices or the asparagus and artichoke hearts and arrange them in an even layer.
- Cover and place the pan in the middle oven rack and bake until the rice is tender and most of the liquid is absorbed, about 30 minutes.

### 5. Top with the peas

- Remove the pan from the oven, uncover the pan, remove the bay leaves, and scatter the peas and chopped olives (optional) over the mixture. Note: Do not stir.
- Cover the pan and let it stand until the peas are heated through and any remaining liquid is absorbed by the rice, about 5 minutes.

### 6. Serve your dish

- Bring the pan immediately to the table and serve directly from the pan.

# Garlicky Shrimp or Mushrooms and Toast with Tomato
## Gambas al Ajillo y Pan con Tomate

We've put together a meal of two popular Spanish tapas (small dishes), also known as bocas or appetizers. The garlicky shrimp and toast with tomatoes are normally eaten at a bar late in the evening and are a great way to explore Spanish cuisine at home. Kids will have fun grating the tomatoes into a pulp! Be adventuresome and sample a Spanish olive oil for fun.

**SERVES**
4

**ALLERGENS**
Dairy-Free, Nut-Free, Gluten-Free Optional, Vegetarian Optional

**TOTAL PREP & COOK TIME**
35 minutes

## What You'll Need

2 pounds medium shrimp

1 lemon

4 garlic cloves

4 plum tomatoes

Rustic crusty bread or gluten-free bread

1½ teaspoons salt

Pepper

2 tablespoons olive oil, plus more as needed

Pinch of red pepper flakes (optional)

## Vegetarian Option

2 pounds mixed button and cremini mushrooms or wild mushrooms

### TOTO TOMATO MIX

2 tablespoons granulated garlic

1 teaspoon dried oregano

1 teaspoon dried basil

### PAPRIKIE HERBIE MIX

1 tablespoon dried parsley

1 teaspoon granulated garlic

1 teaspoon lemon peel granules

1 teaspoon Spanish smoked paprika

## 1. Prep the ingredients ★★

- **Shrimp**—Peel off the shells and remove the tails. Rinse the shrimp.
- **Lemon**—Cut in half, juice half, and save half for another use.
- **Garlic**—Peel and mince or crush using a garlic press.
- **Tomatoes**—Halve.
- **Bread**—Cut into 1-inch slices.
- **Toto Tomato Mix**—Combine all the ingredients in a small bowl and mix well.
- **Paprikie Herbie Mix**—Combine all the ingredients in a small bowl and mix well.

### Vegetarian option

- **Mushrooms**—Rinse and cut into thin slices.

## 2. Prep the toast and assemble the toasts with tomato ★★★

- **Plum tomatoes**—Use the large holes of a grater to grate the flesh side of the tomatoes. Discard the skin and season the tomato pulp with the Toto Tomato Mix, ½ teaspoon of salt, and pepper to taste.
- Adjust the rack to 4 inches below the broiler. Preheat the broiler to high.
- Place the bread slices on a baking sheet and drizzle with olive oil. Broil until crisp, 2 to 3 minutes. Note: Keep a close eye on the broiler so it doesn't burn.
- Spoon the tomato pulp over each slice of toasted bread. Drizzle generously with olive oil and adjust the seasonings to taste.

## 3. Sauté the garlicky shrimp ★★

- In a large skillet, heat the 2 tablespoons of olive oil over medium-high heat until hot.
- Add the minced garlic and sauté until aromatic, about 30 seconds.
- Add the shrimp or mushrooms, Paprikie Herbie Mix, 2 tablespoons of lemon juice, remaining 1 teaspoon of salt, and pepper to taste.
- Sauté until the shrimp are pink and cooked evenly or the mushrooms are browned, 4 to 6 minutes.
- Optional: Add a pinch of red pepper flakes.

## 4. Serve your dish ★

- Divide the shrimp among individual plates and serve with the warm toasts with tomato on the side to sop up the delicious sauce.

# Spanish Omelet with Onion and Bell Pepper
## Tortilla Española

One of the simplest and most beloved dishes in Spain, this recipe features potatoes, onions, and bell peppers mixed with eggs to form a hearty omelet perfect for a snack, lunch, or weekend brunch. According to the book *Culinaria Spain*, tortilla Española has been around since the late 1500s, when it was served to Kings Phillip III and Philip IV of Spain.

**SERVES**
4

**ALLERGENS**
Nut-Free, Gluten-Free, Vegetarian

**TOTAL PREP & COOK TIME**
30 minutes

### What You'll Need

3 medium Yukon Gold potatoes

2 medium onions

1 red bell pepper

2 tablespoons olive oil

6 large eggs

1 teaspoon salt

Pepper

### VIBRANT VEGGIE MIX

1 tablespoon granulated garlic

1 teaspoon dried parsley

1 teaspoon dried tarragon

### 1. Prep the ingredients ★★

- Preheat the oven to 400°F.
- **Potatoes**—Peel and leave whole. Place in a small pot with water covering them by 1 inch.
- **Onions**—Peel and dice.
- **Bell pepper**—Cut in half, discard the stem and seeds, and thinly slice.
- **Vibrant Veggie Mix**—Combine all the ingredients in a small bowl and mix well.

### 2. Boil the potatoes ★★

- Bring the pot with the potatoes to a boil and cook until almost tender, 8 to 10 minutes.
- Drain in a colander. Once cool enough to handle, cut the potatoes into ¼-inch slices.

### 3. Sauté the vegetables (while the potatoes boil) ★★

- In a nonstick skillet, heat 2 tablespoons of olive oil over medium-high heat until hot.
- Add the onions, bell pepper, and Vibrant Veggie Mix and sauté until tender, 3 to 5 minutes.
- Add the sliced potatoes and spread them evenly so the ingredients are all flat.

### 4. Prep the eggs ★

- In a large bowl, whisk the eggs with 1 teaspoon of salt and pepper to taste.

### 5. Bake the omelet ★★

- Pour the egg mixture into the skillet with the vegetables and cook until the bottom begins to firm up, about 2 minutes.
- Place in the oven and bake until the eggs and potatoes are cooked through, 6 to 8 minutes.

### 6. Serve your dish ★

- Run a heatproof rubber spatula around the edges of the pan to loosen the tortilla. Carefully flip it onto a cutting board. Cut into wedges and serve warm.

# Sweden

As the largest country in Northern Europe with four very distinct seasons, Sweden's cuisine is heavily influenced by its climate. Food preservation has been practiced there as early as Viking times, and produce harvested during frost-free months is preserved, stored, and consumed throughout the winter months.

Smaklig måltid!
(SMACK-lee MOHL-teed)
*"Have a tasty meal!" in Swedish*

**YOU'LL COOK:**

**Swedish Meatballs with Pickled Cucumber and Mashed Potatoes (Köttbullar)**

**"Reindeer" Stroganoff with Rice (Renskavspanna)**

**Pea Soup with Swedish Pancakes (Ärtsoppa och Pannkakor)**

**DID YOU KNOW...**

- Anders Celsius, Swedish astronomer extraordinaire, invented the centigrade system and the thermometer that made it work. Zero degrees Celsius = 32 degrees Fahrenheit!

- There are about 100,000 lakes in Sweden ranging in size from little forest ponds to big lakes.

- There is a famous chilly hotel in Sweden! The hugely popular ICEHOTEL in the village of Jukkasjärvi is constructed from scratch each year, with two-ton blocks of ice from the nearby Torne River.

# Swedish Meatballs with Pickled Cucumber and Mashed Potatoes
## Köttbullar

Probably Sweden's most famous dish, these meatballs increased in popularity when the furniture company IKEA introduced them to the world at their in-store restaurants. Ironically, they did not originate in Sweden. The dish was based on a recipe that King Charles XII of Sweden brought back from Turkey in the early 18th century!

**SERVES**
4

**ALLERGENS**
Gluten-Free Optional,
Vegetarian Optional

**TOTAL PREP & COOK TIME**
45 minutes

## What You'll Need

1 onion

4 small cucumbers

2 pounds yellow potatoes

Olive oil

¼ cup apple cider vinegar or white vinegar

1 tablespoon sugar

1 tablespoon plus 2 teaspoons salt

10 peppercorns (optional)

2 teaspoons Dijon mustard (optional)

1 cup milk

4 tablespoons butter, plus more as needed

Pepper

12 ounces ground beef

12 ounces ground pork

¾ cup breadcrumbs or gluten-free breadcrumbs

1 egg

⅔ cup heavy cream

2 teaspoons soy sauce

Mixed berry preserves or lingonberry preserves (optional)

## Vegetarian Option

2 (15-oz) cans lentils

1 cup walnuts

2 tablespoons nutritional yeast (optional)

## OO-LA-LA! GRAVY MIX

1 tablespoon cornstarch

2 teaspoons chicken or vegetable bouillon

½ teaspoon lemon peel granules

1. **Prep the ingredients** ★★
- **Onion**—Peel and dice.
- **Cucumbers**—Trim the ends and cut into thin slices. Place in a bowl with a lid.
- **Potatoes**—Peel and cut into ½-inch pieces. Put into a medium pot and cover with lightly salted water.
- **Oo-la-la! Gravy Mix**—Combine all the ingredients in a small bowl and mix well.
- Lightly grease a baking sheet with oil.

2. **Make the pickled cucumber** ★
- In a small pot over medium-high heat, combine ¼ cup of apple cider vinegar or white vinegar, 1 tablespoon of sugar, 1 tablespoon of salt, peppercorns (optional), and 1 teaspoon of Dijon mustard (optional).
- Bring the mixture to a boil and pour it immediately over the sliced cucumbers.
- Cover the bowl with the lid and set it aside to cool.

3. **Make the mashed potatoes** ★★
- Set the pot of potatoes over medium-high heat and bring to a boil.
- Once boiling, lower the heat to a simmer and cook for another 10 minutes, or until the potatoes are tender.
- Drain the potatoes in a colander and return them to the pot.
- Add ¼ cup of milk and 2 tablespoons of butter.
- Mash, using a potato masher, until smooth. Season with salt and pepper to taste. Note: Add extra butter if you like it creamier.

Continued...

# Swedish Meatballs with Pickled Cucumber and Mashed Potatoes
## Köttbullar

### 4. Prep the meatballs ⭐

- In a small skillet, melt 1 tablespoon of butter or olive oil over medium-high heat.
- Add the diced onion and sauté until soft and golden, about 5 minutes.
- In a large bowl, combine the ground beef, ground pork, sautéed onion, breadcrumbs, remaining ¾ cup of milk, egg, remaining 2 teaspoons of salt, and pepper to taste. Mix well with clean hands.

**Vegetarian option**

- In a food processor, combine the lentils, walnuts, nutritional yeast (optional), sautéed onion, breadcrumbs, remaining ¾ cup of milk, egg, remaining 2 teaspoons of salt, and pepper to taste.
- Form the meat mixture or lentil mixture into 1-inch balls (you can use a small ice cream scoop!).
- Place the meatballs or veggie meatballs on the prepared baking sheet, spacing them out evenly.

### 5. Broil the meatballs ⭐⭐⭐

- Adjust the top oven rack to 6 inches below the broiler. Preheat the broiler to high.
- Place the baking sheet on the top rack of the oven and broil until golden brown, 5 to 6 minutes.
- Flip the meatballs and cook for another 5 to 6 minutes. Be sure to keep an eye on the broiler the entire time so they don't burn.
- Keep warm until ready to serve.

### 6. Serve your dish ⭐⭐

- In a saucepan, melt the remaining 1 tablespoon of butter over medium-high heat.
- Add the Oo-la-la! Gravy Mix and stir for 2 minutes.
- Add 1 cup water, heavy cream, soy sauce, and remaining 1 teaspoon Dijon mustard (optional) and bring to a simmer. Cook until the sauce thickens.
- Place 4 or 5 meatballs on individual plates, top with some gravy, and serve with the pickled cucumber, mashed potatoes, and mixed berries or lingonberry preserves (optional) on the side.

# DID YOU KNOW...

The prestigious Nobel Prizes were established by the Swedish inventor Alfred Nobel. The prizes, awarded annually in fields such as physics, chemistry, medicine, literature, and peace, are presented in Stockholm and Oslo (Peace Prize) on December 10, the anniversary of Nobel's death.

# "Reindeer" Stroganoff with Rice
## Renskavspanna

With roots in the Sámi culture (the Indigenous people in northern Scandinavia), renskavspanna (ren-skav-SPAN-na) was made with thin slices of frozen reindeer meat that had been preserved by burying it in the snow. The meat was pan-fried with wild mushrooms over an open fire. We're sure it was delicious, though here we use beef rib-eye steak instead and cook it on the stove without compromising the taste!

**SERVES**
4

**ALLERGENS**
Nut-Free, Gluten-Free, Vegetarian Optional

**TOTAL PREP & COOK TIME**
50 minutes

### What You'll Need

1 onion

10 ounces button or cremini mushrooms

1½ pounds boneless rib-eye steaks

1½ cups basmati or other long-grain rice

½ teaspoon salt, plus more as needed

4 tablespoons butter

Pepper

8 ounces crème fraîche or heavy cream

1 tablespoon lemon juice

1 cup frozen peas

### Vegetarian Option

1 large leek

20 ounces mixed mushrooms, such as oyster, shiitake, maitake, trumpet (in addition to mushrooms listed to the left)

### BAYISH GARLIC MIX

2 teaspoons granulated garlic

2 teaspoons chicken or vegetable bouillon

2 bay leaves

1. **Prep the ingredients** ★★

- **Onion**—Peel and dice.
- **Mushrooms**—Rinse and thinly slice.
- **Beef**—Freeze for about 20 minutes, or enough to be slightly firmed. Thinly slice or shave the steak against the grain.
- **Bayish Garlic Mix**—Combine all the ingredients in a small bowl and mix well.

**Vegetarian option**

- **Leek**—Trim the root and green part, cut in half lengthwise, thinly slice, and place them in a bowl of water. Any dirt will settle to the bottom of the bowl. Use your hands to break up the leek slices to remove the dirt. Lift the leeks from the water without disturbing the dirt that has settled on the bottom of the bowl.
- **Mixed mushrooms**—Clean and thinly slice.

2. **Cook the rice** ★★

- Rinse the rice in a colander to remove excess starch.
- In a small pot, combine the rice, a pinch of salt, and 2¼ cups water.
- Bring to a boil over medium-high heat.
- Lower the heat, cover, and simmer until the liquid has been absorbed and the rice is tender, about 15 minutes.

3. **Sauté the meat (while the rice is cooking)** ★★

- In a large deep skillet, heat 2 tablespoons of butter over medium-high heat until hot.
- Add the beef and cook over high heat (don't stir) until well browned, about 5 minutes.
- Transfer the meat to a plate.

Continued...

# "Reindeer" Stroganoff with Rice
## Renskavspanna

**4. Cook the mushrooms (while the rice is cooking)** ★★

- In the same skillet, heat the remaining 2 tablespoons of butter or olive oil over medium-high heat until hot.
- Add the diced onion and sliced mushrooms and sauté until the vegetables are slightly dry and brown (don't stir too often), 8 to 10 minutes.
- Add the Bayish Garlic Mix, ½ teaspoon of salt, and pepper to taste. Mix well.

**Vegetarian option**

- Add the diced onion, leeks, and all the sliced mushrooms to the olive oil and sauté until the vegetables are slightly dry and brown, 8 to 10 minutes.
- Add the Bayish Garlic Mix, ½ teaspoon of salt, and pepper to taste. Mix well.

**5. Cook the stroganoff** ★★

- In the same skillet, add the browned meat or mushrooms and ¼ cup water.
- Deglaze the skillet by stirring with a spatula to scrape up the browned bits.
- Add the crème fraîche or heavy cream and lemon juice.
- Lower the heat to a simmer and cook for 10 minutes or until the sauce thickens. Add the frozen peas. Add salt and pepper to taste and cook until the peas are heated through. Remove the bay leaves.

**6. Serve your dish** ★

- Divide the rice among individual plates and top each plate with the stroganoff.

## DID YOU KNOW...

Fika is a Swedish cultural tradition that involves taking a break to enjoy coffee or tea with a sweet treat, often a cinnamon bun or a pastry. It's a cherished social moment for relaxation and connection with others.

# Pea Soup with Swedish Pancakes
## Ärtsoppa och Pannkakor

In Sweden, Thursday is ärtsoppa (airt-soh-pa) and pannkakor (pann-kah-kor) day and it's been a weekly staple there for as long as anyone can remember. There are many stories about the tradition, and one is that Catholics in the Middle Ages served it on Thursdays to fill up before the Friday fast. The classic soup includes salted ham hock or pork knuckle, but in our version, we made it vegetarian. The pancakes are served with whipped cream and preserves for a sweet finish!

**SERVES**
4

**ALLERGENS**
Nut-Free, Gluten-Free Optional, Vegetarian Optional

**TOTAL PREP & COOK TIME**
1 hour 45 minutes + overnight soaking of the split peas

## What You'll Need

1 cup yellow split peas

1 onion

1 large carrot

1 teaspoon salt, plus more as needed

Pepper

3 tablespoons butter, plus more as needed

1¼ cups all-purpose flour or gluten-free flour

2½ cups milk

3 eggs

1 cup heavy whipping cream (optional)

1 tablespoon sugar (optional)

Mixed berry or lingonberry preserves

Grainy brown mustard (optional)

### ÄRTOR MIX

4 teaspoons chicken or vegetable bouillon

¾ teaspoon dried thyme

¾ teaspoon ground ginger

1 bay leaf

1. **Prep the soup ingredients**

- **Split peas**—The night before, rinse and soak the split peas in water to cover the peas by 2 inches.
- **Onion**—Peel and dice.
- **Carrot**—Peel and trim the ends. Cut into small cubes.
- **Ärtor Mix**—Combine all the ingredients in a small bowl and mix well.

2. **Cook the soup**

- Drain the peas in a colander.
- In a large pot, combine the drained split peas, Ärtor Mix, onion, carrot, and 6 cups water and bring to a boil over medium-high heat.
- Once boiling, cover and decrease the heat to low.
- Simmer, stirring occasionally, for 1 to 1½ hours or until the peas are tender.
- Season with salt and pepper to taste.

3. **Prep the pancakes (while the soup is cooking)**

- In a small microwave-safe bowl, melt 3 tablespoons of butter in the microwave for 30 to 40 seconds.
- In a large bowl, combine 1¼ cups of flour, 1 teaspoon of salt, and 1 cup of milk and whisk until smooth.
- Slowly add the remaining 1½ cups of milk. Whisk well.
- Add the eggs and melted butter. Continue whisking until smooth.
- Allow the batter to rest for 20 to 30 minutes.
- Optional: Whipped cream—In a medium bowl, combine the heavy whipping cream and 1 tablespoon of sugar. Whisk until the cream reaches stiff peaks. Store in the refrigerator until ready to serve.

Continued...

# Pea Soup with Swedish Pancakes

## Ärtsoppa och Pannkakor

### 4. Cook the pancakes ★★

- Heat a nonstick skillet over medium-high heat until hot.
- Lightly coat the pan with butter.
- Stir the batter and pour ¼ to ½ cup into the pan to form a thin layer, depending on the size of the pan. Swirl the pan around to coat.
- When the edges of the pancake begin to curl and are lightly browned, about 30 seconds, loosen the pancake with a spatula and flip it over. Cook until golden brown, another 20 to 30 seconds. Transfer the pancake to a plate.
- Repeat with the rest of the batter, making sure to stir the batter before each new pancake. Stack the cooked pancakes on the plate as you go.
- Fold the pancakes in half and then fold again into a small triangle.

### 5. Serve your dish ★

- Ladle the pea soup into individual bowls and serve the pancakes on the side with the mixed berry or lingonberry preserves and whipped cream (optional).
- Optional: Stir grainy brown mustard into the soup for a pop of flavor.

## DID YOU KNOW...

99% of Sweden's waste is recycled.
In 2017, Sweden managed
4,783,000 metric tons of recycling,
which is about 1,042 pounds
per person!

# United Kingdom

There was once a time, as the saying goes, that the sun never set on the British Empire. At its peak in 1920, the British Empire was the largest in history. It controlled so much of the Earth's land area (around 24 percent of the world) that the sun was always shining on at least one of its colonies!

Today, the United Kingdom is much smaller and comprises England, Scotland, Wales, and Northern Ireland. Many of the British Colony countries (also known as Commonwealth countries) are now independent, but they have left their culinary influences on the cuisine of the United Kingdom, as you'll see in the recipes in this chapter.

Dig in!

## YOU'LL COOK:

**Grilled Chicken in Tomato Sauce with Cucumber Yogurt Sauce and Naan (Tikka Masala)**

**Ground Lamb or Beef with Vegetables, Topped with Mashed Potato (Shepherd's Pie)**

**Lamb with Vegetables, Topped with Herby-Garlic Dumplings (Irish Lamb Stew)**

## DID YOU KNOW...

- London was originally a Roman city named Londinium, which was ruled by the Romans from the 1st century to the 5th century. The modern city is now built on top of the Roman ruins.

- The large blue stones of Stonehenge, a famous prehistoric site in England, were brought to their location from Wales, over 160 miles away! Historians still debate how the stones were moved with what little technology humans had at the time.

- The famous New Year's Eve song, "Auld Lang Syne," was originally a Scottish poem written by Robert Burns in 1788. It means "for old times' sake," and the song is all about preserving old friendships and looking back over the events of the year.

# Grilled Chicken in Tomato Sauce with Cucumber Yogurt Sauce and Naan

## Tikka Masala

This tasty dish of marinated and grilled chicken originated in India and immigrants brought it to England. According to folklore, in the 1960s, a British gentleman at a restaurant decided his tikka was too dry, so the chef added a can of tomato soup, spices, and some yogurt, and the sweet and tangy tikka masala was born and became hugely popular. Here, we've given you both options!

 **SERVES**
4

 **ALLERGENS**
Nut-Free, Gluten-Free Optional

 **TOTAL PREP & COOK TIME**
45 minutes + 15 minutes or up to overnight to marinate

## What You'll Need

12 to 20 (6-inch) wooden skewers

2 pounds boneless skinless chicken thighs or pork tenderloin

2 mini cucumbers

1 small red onion

2 medium tomatoes

½ lemon

¾ cup plain yogurt

1 tablespoon tomato paste

2 teaspoons salt

1 teaspoon sugar

Pepper

1½ teaspoons olive oil, plus more as needed

4 naan or gluten-free naan

1 (28-oz) can tomato sauce

½ cup heavy cream

### TIKKAMAS SPICE

2 teaspoons ground cumin

2 teaspoons garam masala

2 teaspoons curry powder

1 teaspoon ground turmeric

1 teaspoon ground ginger

1 teaspoon garlic powder

½ teaspoon paprika

### RAITA HERBIE

1 teaspoon dried mint

1 teaspoon dried cilantro

½ teaspoon garlic powder

## 1. Prep the ingredients and marinate the chicken ★★

- **Wooden skewers**—Soak in a bowl of water for at least 10 minutes.
- **Chicken thighs or pork tender-loin**—Remove any fat and cut into 1½-inch cubes.
- **Cucumbers**—Trim the ends and cut into small cubes.
- **Red onion**—Halve and peel. Cut half the onion into ¼-inch pieces and save the remaining half onion for step 5; soak the diced onion in cold water.
- **Tomatoes**—Cut into ¼-inch cubes.
- **Lemon**—Juice the half lemon.
- **TikkaMas Spice**—Combine all the ingredients in a small bowl and mix well.

## 2. Marinate the chicken or pork ★★

- In a large bowl, combine the chicken or pork, half the TikkaMas Spice, ½ cup of yogurt, 1 table-spoon of tomato paste, 1½ tea-spoons of olive oil, 1½ teaspoons of salt, 1 teaspoon of sugar, and pepper to taste.
- Stir to combine. Let sit for at least 15 minutes or overnight in the refrigerator to maximize the flavors.

## 3. Prep the skewers ★★

- Remove the skewers from the water.
- Place 4 or 5 pieces of marinated chicken or pork on each skewer.
- Brush the chicken or pork with olive oil and place the skewers on a baking sheet.
- Adjust the top oven rack to 6 inches below the broiler. Preheat the broiler to high.
- Broil the skewers until the meat is golden brown, 3 to 4 minutes. Carefully flip the skewers and broil until cooked through, another 3 to 4 minutes.

## 4. Prep the raita and naan ★★

- **Raita Herbie**—Combine all the ingredients in a small bowl and mix well. Preheat the oven to 350°F.
- In a bowl, combine the Raita Herbie, cucumbers, tomatoes, lemon juice, drained diced onion, remaining ¼ cup of yogurt, remaining ½ teaspoon of salt, and pepper to taste. Set aside.
- Brush the naan generously with olive oil. Place on a baking sheet and bake 5 to 7 minutes, or until the naan is warmed through.

## 5. Prep the tikka masala ★★

- In a heavy-bottomed pot, heat 1 tablespoon of olive oil over medi-um-high heat until hot.
- Add the remaining onion and remaining TikkaMas Spice mix. Stir until fragrant, 3 to 5 minutes.
- Add the meat, tomato sauce, ½ cup of heavy cream, ½ teaspoon of sugar, 1 teaspoon of salt, and 1 cup water, and stir to mix well. Lower the heat and simmer for 15 minutes.
- Serve with naan and cucumber raita.

# Ground Lamb or Beef with Vegetables, Topped with Mashed Potato
## Shepherd's Pie

**ALLERGENS**
Nut-Free, Gluten-Free Optional

**TOTAL PREP & COOK TIME**
1 hour 10 minutes

Meat pies, consisting of meat and vegetables simmered in gravy and topped with mashed potatoes, started in England as a way to use left-over Sunday roasts. Although it sometimes is called cottage pie, shepherd's pie is generally made with lamb while cottage pie uses beef. No matter what you call it, this popular dish is found in pubs all over the United Kingdom.

## What You'll Need

1 yellow onion

2 pounds Yukon Gold potatoes

¼ cup milk, plus more as needed

2 tablespoons butter, plus more as needed

1¼ teaspoons salt

Pepper

1 tablespoon olive oil

2 pounds ground lamb or ground beef

2 tablespoons all-purpose flour or cornstarch

2 cups frozen mixed vegetables (such as peas, corn, and carrot mix)

### TOTO WOZTER SAUCE

1 tablespoon Worcestershire sauce

1 tablespoon tomato paste

1 teaspoon granulated garlic

1 teaspoon chicken bouillon

1 teaspoon dried thyme

¼ teaspoon sugar

¼ teaspoon balsamic vinegar

**1. Prep the ingredients** ★★

- Preheat the oven to 400°F.
- **Onion**—Peel and dice.
- **Potatoes**—Peel and cut into ½-inch dice. Put them into a medium pot and cover with lightly salted water.
- **Toto Wozter Sauce**—Combine all the ingredients in a small bowl and mix well.

**2. Cook the potatoes** ★★

- Set the pot of potatoes over medium-high heat and bring to a boil.
- Decrease the heat to a simmer and cook until the potatoes are tender, about 10 minutes.
- Drain the potatoes in a colander and return them to the pot.

**3. Make the mashed potatoes** ★

- Add ¼ cup of milk, 2 tablespoons of butter, ¼ teaspoon of salt, and pepper to taste to the pot with the cooked potatoes.
- Mash the potato mixture, using a potato masher, until smooth. Add more milk and butter if needed to create the consistency you want.

**4. Cook the lamb or beef filling** ★★ **(while the potatoes are boiling)**

- In a large deep skillet, heat 1 tablespoon of olive oil over medium-high heat until hot.
- Add the onion and sauté until tender, 2 to 3 minutes.
- Add the ground lamb or beef, using a fork or wooden spoon to break up the meat, and cook until browned, about 5 minutes.
- Sprinkle the meat with 2 tablespoons of all-purpose flour or cornstarch and toss to coat.
- Add the Toto Wozter Sauce, frozen mixed vegetables, remaining 1 teaspoon of salt, and pepper to taste.
- Cook until the sauce has thickened, 2 to 3 minutes.

**5. Assemble the shepherd's pie** ★

- Spoon the meat filling into a 10-inch pie dish.
- Top the meat filling with the mashed potatoes, spreading it out evenly with a rubber spatula.
- Seal the edges by pushing the mashed potatoes right up to the edge of the baking dish to prevent the mixture from bubbling up as it cooks. (Optional: Use the tines of a fork to make fun designs in the potatoes, like a heart or smiley face.)

**6. Bake and serve your dish** ★★★

- Place the baking dish in the oven and bake until the potatoes begin to brown, about 30 minutes.
- Remove the dish from the oven and let cool for 15 minutes before serving.

# Lamb with Vegetables, Topped with Herby-Garlic Dumplings
## Irish Lamb Stew

Its origins may be in Ireland, but this rich stew full of tender lamb and root vegetables has become all the rage in the United Kingdom, warming tummies everywhere on cold winter nights. It requires slow oven cooking that yields lamb so tender it falls apart. Simple dropped herb dumplings make a nice finishing touch on top of the bubbling stew. For an extra kick, add lots of ground pepper before serving!

 **SERVES**
4

 **ALLERGENS**
Nut-Free, Gluten-Free Optional

 **TOTAL PREP & COOK TIME**
2½ hours

### What You'll Need

2 onions

2 carrots

1 turnip

2 medium potatoes

2½ pounds lamb stew meat

¼ cup pearl barley (optional)

2½ teaspoons salt

Pepper

1 cup all-purpose flour or gluten-free flour

2½ teaspoons baking powder

½ cup milk

1½ tablespoons butter

### STEWIE HERBIE MIX

2 teaspoons chicken bouillon

2 teaspoons dried thyme

2 teaspoons garlic powder

1 teaspoon dried parsley

2 bay leaves

### HERBIE DUMPLING MIX

1 tablespoon dried parsley

1 teaspoon granulated garlic

### 1. Prep the ingredients ★★

- Preheat the oven to 375°F.
- **Onions**—Peel, halve, and thinly slice.
- **Carrots**—Peel, trim the ends, and cut into 1½-inch pieces.
- **Turnip**—Peel, trim the ends, and cut into 1-inch pieces.
- **Potatoes**—Peel, halve, and thinly slice.
- **Stewie Herbie Mix**—Combine all the ingredients in a small bowl and mix well.
- **Herbie Dumpling Mix**—Combine all the ingredients in a small bowl and mix well.

### 2. Layer the lamb and vegetables ★★

- In a Dutch oven or heavy-bottomed pot with a lid, combine the lamb, Stewie Herbie Mix, barley (optional), 4 cups water, 2 teaspoons of salt, and pepper to taste. Combine well.
- Layer the onions, carrots, turnips, and potatoes over the meat.

### 3. Cook the lamb stew ★★

- Cover and place the pot on the middle rack of the oven.
- Bake for 30 minutes. Remove the pot from the oven and stir to mix.
- Return the pot to the oven and bake for 1 more hour, or until the lamb, barley, and vegetables are tender. Add more water, ½ cup at a time, if the stew is too thick.
- Note: If preparing in advance, you may stop at this step. Let the stew cool to room temperature and leave it in the fridge for reheating at a later stage.

### 4. Make the herb dumplings ★★

- In a bowl, combine 1 cup of all-purpose flour or gluten-free flour, 2½ teaspoons baking powder, Herbie Dumpling Mix and ½ teaspoon of salt. Mix well.
- In a saucepan over medium heat, warm ½ cup of milk and 1½ tablespoons of butter until the butter melts.
- Gently pour the milk mixture into the flour mixture and mix thoroughly to form a soft dough.

### 5. Cook the dumplings with the stew ★★

- Remove stew from the oven. Increase the oven temperature to 425°F. Add 1 cup water if the stew is too thick.
- Drop rounded spoonfuls of dumpling dough around the edges of the pot.
- Return the pot to the oven and bake, uncovered, until the dumplings are golden, about 20 minutes.

### 6. Serve your dish ★

- Spoon the stew and herb dumplings into individual bowls.

# Explore Africa

The second largest continent in size and in population, Africa contains 54 countries, according to the United Nations. It is one of the most diverse places on the planet, with a wide variety of terrain, wildlife, and climates, going from desert to rainforest. Africa borders the Atlantic Ocean, the Indian Ocean, the Mediterranean Sea, and the Middle East regions.

The three countries within Africa that are represented in this chapter include:

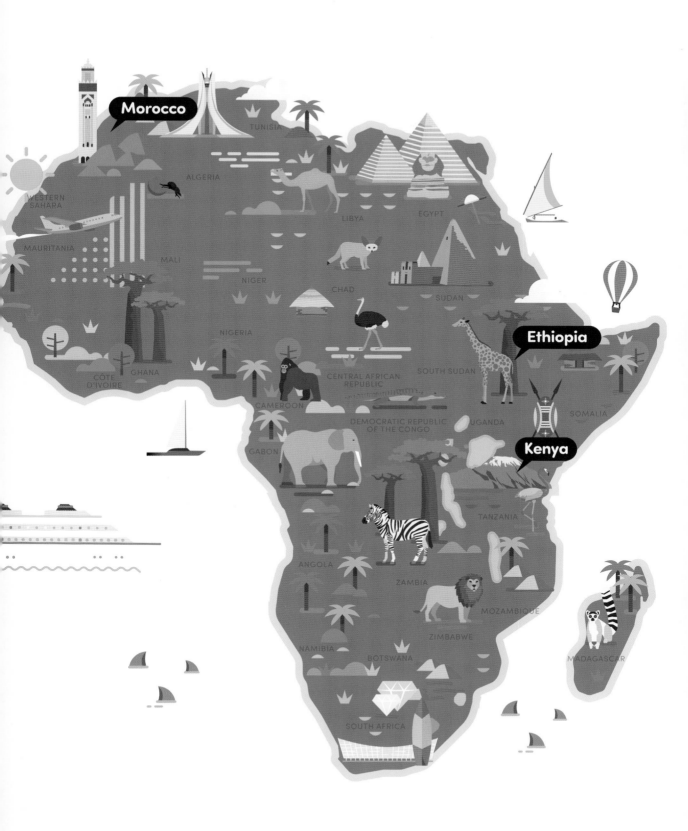

# Kenya

Kenya is a country found in East Africa with a coastline on the Indian Ocean and bordered by South Sudan, Uganda, Somalia, Tanzania, and Ethiopia. Kenya is known for the incredible diversity of its wildlife and national parks. It is home to the "Big Five" game animals: lions, leopards, elephants, buffalo, and rhinoceros.

Furahia Chakula Chako!
(foor-a-hee-a cha-KOO-la cha-ko)
*"Enjoy your meal!" in Swahili*

**YOU'LL COOK:**

**East African Rice with Chicken, Beef, or Vegetables and Kenyan Tomato Salad (Pilau na Kachumbari)**

**Beef or Vegetarian Bean Stew with Cornmeal Mush and Greens (Nyama/Githeri yenye Ugali na Sukuma Wiki)**

**Chicken in Coconut Sauce with Rice and Greens (Kuku Paka)**

# East African Rice with Chicken, Beef, or Vegetables and Kenyan Tomato Salad
## Pilau na Kachumbari

**SERVES**
4

**ALLERGENS**
Dairy-Free, Nut-Free, Gluten-Free, Vegetarian Optional

**TOTAL PREP & COOK TIME**
55 minutes

Pilau (pee-la-ow) can be found in most parts of East Africa, including Kenya. It is a one-pot rice meal cooked with spices and meat, and it is a popular dish for special occasions like public holidays, weddings, and parties. Unlike its Indian counterpart, biryani rice, pilau is less spicy but it's full of flavor! Kachumbari (kah-choo-m-BAH-ree) is a Kenyan tomato salad that goes very well with the pilau.

### What You'll Need

2 pounds boneless skinless chicken thighs or beef stew cubes

1 green bell pepper

3 medium potatoes

6 medium ripe tomatoes

2 red onions

½ lemon

10 sprigs fresh cilantro

2 cups basmati or other long-grain rice

5 tablespoons olive oil

½ teaspoon honey

½ teaspoon salt

Pepper

### Vegetarian Option

8 ounces green beans

1 red bell pepper

1 cup frozen peas

### PILAU SPICE MIX

2 teaspoons ground coriander

2 teaspoons chicken or vegetable bouillon

1 teaspoon ground cumin

1 teaspoon granulated garlic

1 teaspoon ground ginger

½ teaspoon ground cinnamon

¼ teaspoon ground cardamon

¼ teaspoon ground cloves

¼ teaspoon ground turmeric

### 1. Prep the ingredients ★★

- **Chicken or beef**—Trim the fat and cut into 1½- to 2-inch cubes.
- **Green bell pepper**—Cut in half, discard the stem and seeds, and dice.
- **Potatoes**—Peel and cut into ½-inch cubes.
- **Tomatoes**—Cut into ½-inch cubes. Use one-third in step 2 and two-thirds in step 3.
- **Red onion**—Peel and thinly slice. Use three-quarters in step 2 and one-quarter in step 3.
- **Lemon**—Cut in half and juice.
- **Cilantro**—Cut off the stems and rinse well. Finely chop the leaves.
- **Rice**—Rinse the rice in a colander to remove excess starch.
- **Pilau Spice Mix**—Combine all the ingredients in a small bowl and mix well.

#### Vegetarian option

- **Green beans**—Trim the ends and cut into 1-inch pieces.
- **Red bell pepper**—Cut in half, discard the stem and seeds, and dice.

### 2. Prep the pilau rice ★★★

- In a Dutch oven or an ovenproof pan with a lid, heat 3 tablespoons of olive oil over medium-high heat until hot.
- Add three-quarters of the sliced onion and sauté until the onion deeply browns, 6 to 7 minutes. (Be careful not to burn it!)
- Add the Pilau Spice Mix and sauté until fragrant, 1 to 2 minutes.
- **Meat option**: Add the chicken or beef and cook, stirring occasionally, until the meat browns, 5 to 6 minutes.
- **Vegetarian option**: Add the green beans, red bell pepper, and frozen peas and sauté until tender, 1 to 2 minutes.
- Add one-third of the tomatoes, half the green bell pepper, potatoes, rice, and 3 cups water. Stir well to mix.
- Cover the pot tightly with a lid. Decrease the heat to low and cook until the rice is tender and the liquid is absorbed, 20 to 25 minutes.
- Remove from the heat and fluff with a fork to ensure the seasonings are well distributed all around the rice.

### 3. Prep the kachumbari (while the pilau is cooking) ★

- In a serving bowl, combine 1 tablespoon lemon juice, remaining 2 tablespoons of olive oil, ½ teaspoon of honey, ½ teaspoon of salt, and pepper to taste. Whisk well to emulsify.
- Add the remaining diced tomatoes, remaining diced red onion, remaining diced green bell pepper, and 3 tablespoons of chopped cilantro. Toss well.
- Refrigerate the salad until ready to serve.

### 4. Serve your dish ★★

- Spoon the pilau into individual bowls and serve with the kachumbari salad.

# Beef or Vegetarian Bean Stew with Cornmeal Mush and Greens

## Nyama/Githeri yenye Ugali na Sukuma Wiki

 **SERVES**
4

 **ALLERGENS**
Dairy-Free, Nut-Free, Gluten-Free, Vegetarian Optional

 **TOTAL PREP & COOK TIME**
55 minutes

"Nyama" (nee-AH-mah) means "meat" and "ugali" (OO-gah-lee), which is made with white cornmeal, means "mush" in Swahili. Ugali is the most common Kenyan staple and is served with everyday meals alongside vegetables or meat stews. Sukuma wiki (SOO-koo-mah wee-kee) is sautéed kale and spinach and balances out the rest of the meal.

### What You'll Need

2 yellow onions

8 ounces fresh kale

8 ounces fresh spinach

2½ pounds beef stew cubes

1½ teaspoons salt, plus more as needed

Pepper

3 tablespoons oil

1 (14.5-oz) can crushed tomatoes

½ cup milk

3 tablespoons butter

1¼ cups white cornmeal

### Vegetarian Option

1 (15-oz) can red kidney beans

1 (15-oz) can pinto beans

1 carrot

1 cup frozen corn

### NYAMA MIX

2 teaspoons granulated garlic

2 teaspoons vegetable or beef bouillon

2 teaspoons curry powder

2 teaspoons dried cilantro

1 teaspoon paprika

### 1. Prep the ingredients ★★

- **Onions**—Peel and dice. Use three-quarters in step 3 and one-quarter in step 5.
- **Kale**—Rinse. Separate the center ribs from the leaves and discard them. Roughly chop the leaves.
- **Spinach**—Rinse. Trim the ends and roughly chop.
- **Nyama Mix**—Combine all the ingredients in a small bowl and mix well.

**Vegetarian option**

- **Kidney beans and pinto beans**—Drain and rinse the beans in a colander.
- **Carrot**—Peel, trim the ends, and cut into ½-inch cubes.

### 2. Brown the meat ★★

- Season the beef with 1 teaspoon of salt and pepper to taste.
- In a Dutch oven or heavy-bottomed pot, heat 2 tablespoons of oil over medium-high heat until hot.
- Add the seasoned beef and sear until browned, 4 to 5 minutes per side. Place the beef on a plate.

### 3. Prep the stew ★★

- In the same Dutch oven or heavy-bottomed pot, add the remaining 1 tablespoon of oil and three-quarters of the diced onion. Sauté until soft, about 1 minute.
- Add the Nyama Mix and stir continuously until fragrant, 2 to 3 minutes.
- Add the browned beef, crushed tomatoes, and 1 cup water.

**Vegetarian option**

- Add the red kidney beans, pinto beans, diced carrot, frozen corn, crushed tomatoes, and 1 cup water.
- Bring to a boil, turn the heat to low, and simmer until the beef is tender, 40 to 45 minutes, or until the beans and vegetables are tender, 10 to 15 minutes. Add salt and pepper to taste.

### 4. Prep the ugali ★★

- In a large pot over medium-high heat, combine 1½ cups water, ½ cup milk or water, the remaining 2 tablespoons of oil, and a pinch of salt and bring to a boil.
- Add the cornmeal to the pot, a little bit at a time, stirring constantly.
- Lower the heat and continue to cook, stirring every minute or so, until the cornmeal is thick and cooked through, 12 to 15 minutes.

### 5. Cook the sukuma wiki ★★

- In a large skillet, heat 3 tablespoons of butter over medium-high heat until melted.
- Add the remaining diced onion and sauté for about 3 minutes.
- Add the chopped kale and spinach and sauté until tender, 3 to 5 minutes. Don't overcook the spinach.
- Add the remaining ½ teaspoon of salt and pepper to taste.

### 6. Serve your dish ★

- Serve the stew with the ugali and sukuma wiki on the side. Eat with your hands like Kenyans do—no utensils needed!

# Chicken in Coconut Sauce with Rice and Greens

## Kuku Paka

Kuku paka ("kuku" is Swahili for "chicken" and "paka" is Bengali for "delicious") is a popular Kenyan coastal dish that represents the country's many cultural influences, from African to European to Indian. It requires grilling the marinated meat before braising it in a spiced coconut sauce. Sukuma wiki, this time made with kale, is a great side dish here.

 **SERVES**
4

 **ALLERGENS**
Dairy-Free, Nut-Free, Gluten-Free, Vegetarian Optional

 **TOTAL PREP & COOK TIME**
45 minutes + 1 to 5 hour marinate time

## What You'll Need

2 medium tomatoes

10 ounces fresh kale

1 large onion

½ lemon

4 sprigs fresh cilantro (optional)

4 chicken drumsticks and 4 thighs

2½ teaspoons salt, plus more as needed

Pepper

3 tablespoon olive oil, plus more as needed

1 (15-oz) can coconut milk

1½ cups basmati or other long-grain rice

### Vegetarian Option

2 (16-oz) packages firm tofu

1 red bell pepper

### KUKUPAKA MIX

2 teaspoons granulated garlic

2 teaspoons ground cumin

1 teaspoon ground coriander

1 teaspoon ground turmeric

1 teaspoon ground ginger

1 teaspoon chili powder

1 teaspoon vegetarian or chicken bouillon

1. **Prep the ingredients** ★★
- **Tomatoes**—Dice.
- **Kale**—Rinse. Separate the center ribs from the leaves and discard them. Roughly chop the leaves.
- **Onion**—Peel and dice. Use three-quarters in step 2 and one-quarter in step 5.
- **Lemon**—Juice the half lemon.
- **Cilantro (optional)**—Cut off the stems and rinse well. Finely chop the leaves.
- **Kukupaka Mix**—Combine all the ingredients in a small bowl and mix well.

**Vegetarian option**
- **Tofu**—Drain. Use paper towels to press out the liquid from the tofu. Cut into 1-inch cubes.
- **Red bell pepper**—Cut in half, discard the stem and seeds, and dice.

2. **Marinate the chicken and prep the coconut sauce (Note: marinate for at least 1 hour)** ★★
- Using a food processor or blender, combine the diced tomatoes, three-quarters of the diced onion, Kukupaka Mix, 2 teaspoons of salt, and pepper to taste. Blend into a paste.
- Rub one-third of the paste all over the chicken pieces or tofu and marinate in the refrigerator for at least 1 hour, or up to 5 hours. Reserve the remaining paste for the sauce.
- In a deep skillet, heat 1 tablespoon of oil over medium-high heat. Add the remaining paste and cook, stir occasionally, until all the moisture evaporates, 5 to 10 minutes. The paste should be thick and dark.
- Turn down the heat, add the coconut milk and 1 cup water, and simmer for 5 minutes. Turn off the heat.

3. **Cook the rice** ★★
- Rinse the rice in a colander to remove excess starch.
- In a small pot, combine the rice, a pinch of salt, and 2¼ cups water.
- Bring to a boil over medium-high heat. Lower the heat, cover, and simmer until the liquid has been absorbed and the rice is tender, about 15 minutes.
- Remove from the heat, fluff the cooked rice with a fork, and keep warm until ready to serve.

Continued...

# Chicken in Coconut Sauce with Rice and Greens
## Kuku Paka

**4. Cook the kuku paka** ★★

- Adjust the top oven rack to 6 inches below the broiler. Preheat the broiler to high.
- Cover a baking sheet with aluminum foil and lightly grease it with oil.
- Spread out the marinated chicken or tofu on the prepared baking sheet.
- Broil for 5 to 6 minutes per side for chicken or 2 to 3 minutes for tofu, or until dark brown and slightly charred.
- Add the broiled chicken or tofu, bell pepper, and 1 teaspoon lemon juice to the coconut sauce. Turn the heat to low, cover, and simmer for 5 to 6 minutes.
- Taste the sauce and adjust the seasoning with salt and pepper to taste.

**5. Prep the sukuma wiki (while the kuku paka is cooking)** ★★

- In a large skillet, heat the remaining 2 tablespoons of olive oil over medium-high heat.
- Add the remaining diced onion and sauté for about 3 minutes.
- Add the chopped kale and sauté for 3 to 5 minutes. Don't overcook or it will get mushy.
- Add the remaining ½ teaspoon of salt and pepper to taste.

**6. Serve your dish** ★

- Garnish the chicken with chopped cilantro (optional) and serve with the rice and sukuma wiki on the side.

## DID YOU KNOW...

Kenya is part of the annual Great Migration, where millions of wildebeests, zebras, and other animals cross the Serengeti-Mara ecosystem in search of fresh grazing grounds.

# Ethiopia

Ethiopia is Africa's oldest independent country (founded in 980 BCE) and the second largest by population. It is a landlocked country bordered by Djibouti, Eritrea, Kenya, Somalia, South Sudan, Sudan, and Somalia.

መልካም ማዕድ!
Melikami migibi
(MEL-kahm MEE-gib)
*"Good feasting!" in Amharic*

**YOU'LL COOK:**

**Spicy Chicken or Vegetable Stew with Salad and Ethiopian Flatbread (Doro Wat be Injera)**

**Sautéed Beef, Chicken, or Vegetables with Rice and Collard Greens (Tibs Wot ena Gomen Wat)**

**Red Lentil Stew over Rice (Misir Wat)**

**DID YOU KNOW...**

- Ethiopia is the only African country never colonized by any European country.

- Ethiopia runs on its own calendar—it observes 13 calendar months per year! This makes the Ethiopian calendar 7 years behind the rest of the world!

- Around 70 percent of Africa's mountains are in Ethiopia.

# Spicy Chicken or Vegetable Stew with Salad and Ethiopian Flatbread
## Doro Wat be Injera

Ethiopian food is often served on a communal platter with a layer of flatbread called injera (in-JEH-rah) and four or five dishes on top. To eat, you use your hands to tear off pieces of injera and scoop up bites of the stew or vegetables (no utensils needed!). Injera is usually made with a batter that is fermented for 4 or 5 days, but for this recipe we use active dry yeast to speed up the process.

**SERVES**
4

**ALLERGENS**
Nut-Free, Gluten-Free Optional, Vegetarian Optional

**TOTAL PREP & COOK TIME**
1 hour 25 minutes + overnight fermentation

## What You'll Need

4 eggs

1 lemon

1½ pounds boneless skinless chicken thighs

4 medium onions

½ head butter lettuce

1 cup cherry tomatoes

5 tablespoons butter or oil, plus more as needed

1½ teaspoons salt

Pepper

2 tablespoons olive oil

1 teaspoon honey

## Vegetarian Option

1 eggplant

¼ head cauliflower

1 (15-oz) can chickpeas, drained

## INJERA MIX

1 cup all-purpose flour or gluten-free flour

1 cup teff flour

1 teaspoon active yeast

¼ teaspoon salt

## DORO WAT SPICE MIX

1½ teaspoons paprika

1 teaspoon chicken or vegetable bouillon

¾ teaspoon ground coriander

¾ teaspoon garlic powder

½ teaspoon fenugreek

¼ teaspoon ground cardamon

¼ teaspoon ground allspice

¼ teaspoon ground cinnamon

¼ teaspoon ground ginger

¼ teaspoon ground nutmeg

¼ teaspoon ground cumin

⅛ teaspoon chili powder

1. **Prep the injera bread (requires overnight fermentation)**

- **Injera Mix**—In a large bowl, combine 1 cup of all-purpose flour, 1 cup of teff flour, 1 teaspoon of active yeast, and ¼ teaspoon of salt and mix well. Add 2½ cups warm water and stir well until combined.
- Cover loosely with a paper towel and let stand at room temperature, undisturbed, overnight.
- Place the eggs in a saucepan, add enough cold water to cover them, and bring to a boil over medium-high heat.
- Turn off the heat, cover the pan with a lid, and let sit for 10 minutes. When cool, drain and peel the eggs. Refrigerate the eggs until ready to use.

2. **Prep the ingredients**

- **Lemon**—Cut in half and juice. Save 1 tablespoon for step 5; use the remaining juice to marinate the chicken.
- **Chicken**—Cut into 1-inch pieces. Place in a bowl with the remaining lemon juice and mix well. Let marinate.
- **Onions**—Peel. Using a grater, shred the onions. If using a food processor, chop the onions roughly and quickly (not too fine).
- **Lettuce**—Roughly chop.
- **Tomatoes**—Cut in half.
- **Doro Wat Spice Mix**—Combine all the ingredients in a small bowl and mix well.

**Vegetarian option**

- **Eggplant**—Peel, trim the ends, and cut into 1-inch cubes.
- **Cauliflower**—Trim the ends and cut into small florets.

3. **Make the stew**

- In a Dutch oven or heavy-bottomed pot, heat 4 tablespoons of butter or oil over medium-high heat until melted.
- Add the onions and cook until golden brown, about 10 minutes.
- Add the Doro Wat Spice Mix and marinated chicken or vegetables and chickpeas.
- Sauté for 10 minutes. Add 2 cups water, 1 teaspoon of salt, and pepper to taste. Bring to a boil, then to decrease the heat to a simmer and cook until the chicken or vegetables are tender, about 20 minutes. Add the hard-boiled eggs and simmer until warmed through, about 5 minutes.

Continued...

# Spicy Chicken or Vegetable Stew with Salad and Ethiopian Flatbread

## Doro Wat with Injera

**4. Prep the Injera bread (while the stew is simmering)** ★★

- Preheat the oven to the lowest setting.
- Gently stir the injera batter. It should resemble pancake batter, with slight bubbles.
- In a large nonstick skillet, heat the remaining 1 tablespoon of butter or oil over medium-high heat until hot.
- Working in batches, add ¾ cup injera batter to the skillet. Gently swirl the skillet to spread out the batter.
- Cook on one side only for about 2 minutes. Gently transfer the injera flatbread to a baking sheet and keep warm in the oven until ready to serve. Repeat with the remaining injera batter, adding more butter as needed.

**5. Prep the salad** ★

- In a serving bowl, combine the remaining 1 tablespoon of lemon juice, 2 tablespoons of olive oil, 1 teaspoon of honey, remaining ½ teaspoon of salt, and pepper to taste. Whisk well to emulsify. Add the chopped lettuce and cherry tomatoes. Toss well.

**6. Serve your dish** ★

- Place the injera flatbread on a large platter. Top it with the doro wat stew, letting the sauce soak into the bread. Serve with the salad on the side. Eat communally with your hands, no utensils needed!

## DID YOU KNOW...

Ethiopia is widely regarded as the birthplace of coffee. Legend has it that a goat herder named Kaldi discovered coffee after noticing the energizing effects it had on his goats when they ate the coffee cherries.

# Sautéed Beef, Chicken, or Vegetables with Rice and Collard Greens

## Tibs Wot ena Gomen Wat

Tibs wot is a stir-fried dish made with beef or chicken. Because the meat is thinly sliced, it is quick to prepare. As with other Ethiopian dishes, it is served traditionally with injera bread, though here we decided to serve it over rice, which makes it a good weeknight meal. Accompany it with gomen wat, which is made with collard greens or kale, and seasoned with lime juice.

**SERVES**
4

**ALLERGENS**
Nut-Free, Gluten-Free, Vegetarian Optional

**TOTAL PREP & COOK TIME**
55 minutes + 20 minutes to overnight marinate time

## What You'll Need

- 1½ pounds sirloin steak or boneless skinless chicken breasts
- 1 large onion
- 1 large tomato
- 1 lime
- 1 bunch collard greens or kale
- 1½ cups basmati or other long-grain rice
- 2 teaspoons salt, plus more as needed
- 1 tablespoon olive oil
- Pepper
- 4 tablespoons butter or oil

### Vegetarian Option

- ½ head cabbage
- 1 carrot

### GOMEN SPICE MIX

- 2 teaspoons garlic powder
- 1 teaspoon ground ginger
- 1 teaspoon onion powder
- 1 teaspoon paprika

### TIBS WOT RUB

- 2 teaspoons paprika
- 1 teaspoon chicken or vegetable bouillon
- ¾ teaspoon ground coriander
- ¾ teaspoon garlic powder
- 1/4 teaspoon fenugreek
- ¼ teaspoon ground cardamon
- ¼ teaspoon ground allspice
- ¼ teaspoon ground cinnamon
- ¼ teaspoon ground ginger
- ¼ teaspoon ground nutmeg
- ¼ teaspoon ground cumin
- Pinch of chili powder

1. **Prep the ingredients** ⭐⭐

- **Steak or chicken**—Cut into ¼-inch slices. In a medium bowl, combine the steak or chicken with the Tibs Wot Rub and mix well to thoroughly coat. Marinate for 20 minutes or overnight in the fridge.
- **Onion**—Peel and dice.
- **Tomato**—Cut into ½-inch cubes.
- **Lime**—Cut in half and juice. Use half in step 3 and the remaining half in step 4.
- **Collard greens or kale**—Separate the center ribs from the leaves and discard them. Roughly chop the leaves.
- **Tibs Wot Rub**—Combine all the ingredients in a small bowl and mix well.
- **Gomen Spice mix**—Combine all the ingredients in a small bowl and mix well.

**Vegetarian option**

- **Cabbage**—Remove the core and cut the cabbage into ¼-inch slices.
- **Carrot**—Peel, trim the ends, and cut into ¼-inch slices.

2. **Cook the rice** ⭐⭐

- Rinse the rice in a colander to remove excess starch.
- In a small pot, combine the rice, a pinch of salt, and 2¼ cups water. Bring to a boil over medium-high heat.
- Lower the heat, cover, and simmer until the liquid has been absorbed and the rice is tender, about 15 minutes.
- Remove from the heat, fluff the cooked rice with a fork, and keep warm until ready to serve.

3. **Prep and cook the gomen wat (while the rice is cooking)** ⭐⭐

- In a large skillet, heat 1 tablespoon of olive oil over medium-high heat until hot.
- Add the chopped collard greens or kale and the Gomen Spice Mix. Sauté until the leaves start to wilt, 3 to 5 minutes.
- Add half the lime juice, 1 teaspoon of salt, and pepper to taste. Cover and cook until the greens are tender, another 7 to 10 minutes.

Continued...

# Sautéed Beef, Chicken, or Vegetables with Rice and Collard Greens

## Tibs Wot ena Gomen Wat

4. **Cook the tibs wot (while the rice is cooking)** ★★★

- In a large skillet, heat 2 tablespoons of butter or oil over medium heat until hot.
- Add the onion and tomato and sauté until tender, 3 to 5 minutes.
- Add the sliced steak or chicken, the remaining lime juice, the remaining 1 teaspoon of salt, and pepper to taste.

**Vegetarian option**

- Add the cabbage, carrot, and Tibs Wot Rub.
- Sauté over medium-high heat until the meat or vegetables are cooked through, 7 to 10 minutes. Stir in the remaining 2 tablespoons of butter at the end.
- If the pan looks dry, add water, 1 tablespoon at a time. Use a wooden spoon to scrape up any brown bits from the bottom of the pan.

5. **Serve your dish** ★

- Serve the tibs wot over rice with the gomen wat on the side.

## DID YOU KNOW...

Ethiopia is home to the highest peak in Africa, Mount Ras Dashen. Standing at an elevation of 4,550 meters (14,928 feet), it is part of the Simien Mountains.

# Red Lentil Stew over Rice
## Misir Wat

Piping-hot vegetable stew over hearty brown rice is the ultimate comfort food! Misir wat is a stew anchored with lentils, seasoned with berbere spices, and served on injera flatbread. In our version, we serve it over rice, which is faster to cook, so it makes a nice weekday meal. The lentils plus sweet potato and spinach make this a vegetarian stew that is packed with nutrients.

**SERVES**
4

**ALLERGENS**
Nut-Free, Gluten-Free,
Vegetarian Optional

**TOTAL PREP & COOK TIME**
50 minutes

### What You'll Need

1 sweet potato

1 large onion

6 ounces spinach

¾ cup red or green lentils

2 tablespoons butter

1 (15-oz) can crushed tomatoes

½ teaspoon sugar

1½ teaspoons salt, plus
more as needed

1½ cups quick-cooking brown rice

### MISIR WAT SPICE MIX

2 teaspoons paprika

1 teaspoon chicken or
vegetable bouillon

¾ teaspoon ground coriander

¾ teaspoon garlic powder

¼ teaspoon fenugreek

¼ teaspoon ground cardamon

¼ teaspoon ground allspice

¼ teaspoon ground cinnamon

¼ teaspoon ground ginger

¼ teaspoon ground nutmeg

¼ teaspoon ground cumin

Pinch of chili powder

### 1. Prep the ingredients ★★

- **Sweet potato**—Peel and cut into ¼-inch dice.
- **Onion**—Peel and dice.
- **Spinach**—Thinly slice.
- **Lentils**—Rinse in a colander under cold running water and set aside.
- **Misir Wat Spice Mix**—Combine all the ingredients in a small bowl and mix well.

### 2. Cook the misir wat ★★

- In a Dutch oven or heavy-bottomed pot, heat 2 tablespoons of butter or oil over medium-high heat until hot.
- Add the onion and Misir Wat Spice Mix and sauté until tender, about 5 minutes.
- Add the red or green lentils, sweet potatoes, crushed tomatoes, ½ teaspoon of sugar, and 1½ teaspoon of salt.
- Add 2 cups water and bring to a boil. Lower the heat, cover, and simmer until the sweet potatoes and lentils are tender, 20 to 25 minutes.
- Add more water, a little at a time, if the sauce gets thick and dry.
- Add the spinach and simmer until the spinach has wilted, about 2 minutes.

### 3. Cook the brown rice (while the misir wat is simmering) ★★

- Rinse the rice in a colander to remove excess starch.
- In a small pot, combine the rice, a pinch of salt, and 2¼ cups water. Bring to a boil over medium-high heat.
- Lower the heat, cover, and simmer until the liquid has been absorbed and the rice is tender, about 15 minutes.
- Remove from the heat, fluff the cooked rice with a fork, and keep warm until ready to serve.

### 4. Serve your dish ★

- Spoon the rice into individual bowls and top with the misir wat.

# Morocco

Found on the northwest coast of Africa, Morocco has a long history of immigration, invasion, and colonization that has shaped its cuisine. Its first inhabitants, the Berbers, used local ingredients, such as olives, figs, and dates, to prepare meat stews. The Arabs introduced spices (cinnamon, ginger, saffron, cumin, caraway) and bread. Persians, Moors, French, British, and Spanish have also left their marks on Moroccan cuisine.

بالصحة
bessha
(be-saha)
*"To your health!" in Arabic*

**YOU'LL COOK:**

**Butternut Squash, Cauliflower, and Chickpea Stew (Tagine)**

**Lamb Kebabs with Potato and Zucchini Pancakes (Brochettes d'Agneau/Kabab Lhaml)**

**Spiced Lamb or Chicken Flatbread with Tomato and Mint (Khobza Medfouna)**

**DID YOU KNOW...**

- M'Goun Valley in Morocco produces 3,000 to 4,000 tons of wild roses every year and is also known as the Vallée des Roses. Most of these roses are used by French perfume companies.

- There is a "Red City" and a "Blue City" in Morocco. The city of Chefchaouen is known as the Blue Pearl of Morocco because the entire medina (the old historic district) and a large portion of the mountain village is painted pale blue. The city of Marrakesh is called the Red City due to the reddish hue of the clay and sandstone used to construct many of the old buildings there.

# Butternut Squash, Cauliflower, and Chickpea Stew
## Moroccan Tagine

A tagine is a North African dish cooked in an earthenware pot of the same name, which has a wide, shallow base, a tall conical lid, and is sometimes referred to as a "maraq." As the food cooks, steam rises into the cone, condenses, and then trickles down the sides back into the dish, creating a uniquely moist and hot cooking environment. If you don't have a tagine, you can get nearly the same effect by using a Dutch oven or a heavy pot with a lid.

**SERVES**
4

**ALLERGENS**
Dairy-Free, Nut-Free, Vegetarian

**TOTAL PREP & COOK TIME**
45 minutes

### What You'll Need

1 pound cauliflower (about ½ head)

1 pound butternut squash (1 small butternut squash)

1 yellow onion

1 (15-oz) can chickpeas

1 tablespoon plus 1 teaspoon olive oil

1 (15-oz) can diced tomatoes

1½ teaspoons salt, plus more as needed

Pepper

¾ cup couscous

¼ cup sliced almonds (optional)

### SAVORY TAGINE MIX

1½ tablespoons dried parsley

2½ teaspoons vegetable bouillon

2 teaspoons ground cumin

1 teaspoon sweet paprika

1 teaspoon granulated garlic

1 teaspoon ground turmeric

1 teaspoon ground coriander

1 teaspoon ground ginger

½ teaspoon ground cinnamon

½ teaspoon ground cardamon

½ teaspoon sugar

1. **Prep the ingredients**

- **Cauliflower**—Remove the core and discard. Cut into small florets.
- **Butternut squash**—Peel and cut into 1-inch pieces.
- **Onion**—Peel and dice.
- **Chickpeas**—Drain in a colander.
- **Savory Tagine Mix**—Combine all the ingredients in a small bowl and mix well.

2. **Prep the tagine**

- In a large heavy-bottomed pot or Dutch oven, heat 1 tablespoon of olive oil over medium-high heat.
- Add the onion and Savory Tagine Mix and sauté until the onion is tender and fragrant, about 5 minutes.
- Add the butternut squash, diced tomatoes, and 2 cups water and bring to a boil. Lower the heat to medium and simmer for 10 minutes.
- Add the cauliflower florets, chickpeas, 1 teaspoon of salt, and pepper to taste.
- Cover and simmer until tender, 5 to 7 minutes. Taste, and add more salt and pepper as needed.

3. **Make the couscous (while the tagine is cooking)**

- In a medium saucepan, combine the couscous, 1 cup water, remaining ½ teaspoon of salt, and remaining 1 teaspoon of olive oil and bring to a boil. Cover and remove from the heat.
- Let stand for 5 minutes, then fluff with a fork.
- Cover and keep warm until ready to serve.

4. **Serve your dish**

- Spoon the couscous into individual bowls and top with the tagine.
- Optional: Garnish with slivered almonds.

# Lamb Kebabs with Potato and Zucchini Pancakes
## Brochettes d'Agneau/Kabab Lhaml

The best Moroccan food is street food! One of the most delicious examples is lamb kebabs. To find them, just follow the billowing clouds of smoke in the medina and you'll be rewarded with mouthwatering kebabs cooking over charcoal. In this version, the meat is marinated in spices, skewered along with vegetables, and then broiled in the oven. Kids will have fun assembling the kebabs and creating interesting patterns!

**SERVES**
4

**ALLERGENS**
Dairy-Free, Nut-Free,
Vegetarian Optional

**TOTAL PREP & COOK TIME**
40 minutes

### What You'll Need

8 wooden skewers

1 large red onion

1 lemon

3 tablespoons olive oil, plus more as needed

½ teaspoon sugar

3 teaspoons salt

Pepper

2 pounds cubed lamb stew meat

2 medium potatoes

1 medium zucchini

1 large egg

3 tablespoons all-purpose flour

1 cup cherry tomatoes

### Vegetarian Option

2 medium zucchini

6 ounces button mushrooms

2 bell peppers, any color

### SHISH KEBABIN' MIX

1 tablespoon ground cumin

1 tablespoon ground coriander

1 tablespoon dried mint

2 teaspoons granulated garlic

1½ teaspoons sweet paprika

¼ teaspoon lemon peel granules

### 1. Prep the ingredients ★★

- **Skewers**—Submerge them in water and soak for at least 10 minutes.
- **Red onion**—Peel and cut into 1-inch slices.
- **Lemon**—Halve and juice.
- **Shish Kebabin' Mix**—Combine all the ingredients in a small bowl and mix well.

#### Vegetarian option

- **Zucchini**—Trim the ends and cut into 1½-inch pieces.
- **Mushrooms**—Rinse.
- **Bell peppers**—Remove the stem and seeds and cut into 1½-inch pieces.

### 2. Marinate the lamb or vegetables ★★

- In a medium bowl, combine the Shish Kebabin' Mix, lemon juice, 2 tablespoons of olive oil, ½ teaspoon of sugar, 2 teaspoons of salt, and pepper to taste and whisk to mix.
- Add the lamb cubes or Vegetarian Option vegetables to the marinade. Let sit for at least 15 minutes or cover and refrigerate overnight.

### 3. Prep the pancakes ★★

- **Potatoes**—Peel and grate.
- **Zucchini**—Trim the ends, discard, and grate.
- Wrap the grated potatoes and zucchini in paper towels and squeeze out as much liquid as possible.
- In a large bowl, combine the grated potato and zucchini mixture, egg, 3 tablespoons of flour, remaining 1 teaspoon of salt, and pepper to taste.

### 4. Cook the pancakes ★★

- In a large nonstick skillet, heat the remaining 1 tablespoon of olive oil over medium-high heat until hot.
- Add 2 tablespoons of the potato and zucchini mixture per pancake to the skillet. Flatten with a fork and lower the heat to medium.
- Cook until the edges are golden brown, 1 to 2 minutes per side. Place the cooked pancakes on a platter and cover with aluminum foil to keep warm.
- Repeat with the remaining potato and zucchini mixture. Add more oil as needed to keep the pancakes from sticking.

### 5. Skewer and broil the kebabs ★

- Lightly grease a baking sheet with olive oil.
- Toss the cherry tomatoes and red onion with the marinated lamb or vegetables.
- Thread the meat and vegetables onto skewers, creating a pleasing pattern. Place the skewers on the prepared baking sheet.
- Adjust the top oven rack to 6 inches below the broiler. Preheat the broiler to high.
- Broil until the meat and vegetables are slightly browned, 4 to 5 minutes per side. Watch carefully, as it's very easy to burn them under the broiler.

### 6. Serve your dish ★

- Place 2 pancakes on each plate along with 2 kebabs.

# Spiced Lamb or Chicken Flatbread with Tomato and Mint

## Khobza Medfouna

There is nothing more delicious than flatbread that's bursting with savory Middle Eastern flavors and textures! Kids will love rolling out their own dough, spreading the tomato sauce, and topping them with spiced lamb and grated mozzarella to create these Moroccan pizzas. If you choose to make the dough from scratch, you'll need to add 2 hours to the prep time, but the kids will love it.

**SERVES**
4

**ALLERGENS**
Nut-Free,
Vegetarian Optional

**TOTAL PREP & COOK TIME**
30 minutes + 2 hours if making dough from scratch

## What You'll Need

### Flatbread

2¼ cups all-purpose flour, plus more as needed

2 tablespoons olive oil

1 teaspoon salt

1 teaspoon sugar

2¼ teaspoons instant yeast

OR

2 balls prepared pizza dough

1 medium onion

3 medium tomatoes

½ cup fresh mint or 3 tablespoons dried mint

1 tablespoon olive oil

1 pound ground lamb or chicken

½ teaspoon sugar

½ teaspoon salt, plus more as needed

1 (15-oz) can tomato sauce

8 ounces grated mozzarella cheese

Red pepper flakes (optional)

### Vegetarian Option

2 medium eggplants

### ROCKIN' MOROCCAN SPICE

1½ teaspoons ground cumin

1 teaspoon ground cinnamon

1 teaspoon paprika

1 teaspoon garlic powder

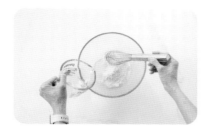

**1. Optional: Make the flatbread from scratch** ★

- In a large bowl, combine the 2¼ cups of flour, 2 tablespoons of olive oil, 1 teaspoon of salt, 1 teaspoon of sugar, yeast, and ¾ cup warm water. Mix well with clean hands.
- Lightly flour a clean surface. Transfer the dough to the floured surface and knead until smooth and elastic, 8 to 10 minutes.
- Transfer the dough to an oiled bowl and cover with plastic wrap. Set aside in a warm area to rise until it doubles in size, 1½ to 2 hours.
- If not making the dough from scratch, bring the balls of prepared dough to room temperature.

**2. Prep the ingredients** ★★

- **Onion**—Peel and dice.
- **Tomatoes**—Cut in half, remove the seeds, and cut into small cubes.
- **Fresh mint (optional)**—Finely chop.
- **Rockin' Moroccan Spice**—Combine all the ingredients in a small bowl and mix well.

**Vegetarian option**

- **Eggplant**—Trim the ends, peel, and cut into ¼-inch cubes.

**3. Sauté the meat or eggplant** ★★

- In a large skillet, heat 1 tablespoon of olive oil over medium-high heat until hot.
- Add the onion and sauté until tender and lightly browned, about 3 minutes.
- Add the meat or eggplant, Rockin' Moroccan Spice, ½ teaspoon of sugar, and ½ teaspoon of salt and cook, using a fork to crumble the meat, until cooked through, about 5 minutes.

**4. Prep the flatbread dough** ★★

- Preheat the oven to 450°F.
- Line a baking sheet with parchment paper and sprinkle it generously with flour.
- Cut the dough into 2 portions. Lightly flour a clean surface and gently stretch each piece of dough into a 7-by-14-inch rectangle. Place the dough on 2 baking sheets.

**5. Assemble and bake the flatbread** ★★

- Using a large spoon or spatula, spread the tomato sauce evenly over the dough, leaving a ½-inch border all the way around.
- Spread out the meat or eggplant mixture over the sauce and sprinkle with the mozzarella cheese.
- Bake until the center is cooked through and the dough is golden brown and crisp, 8 to 12 minutes.

**6. Serve the dish** ★

- In a bowl, toss the diced tomatoes, mint, and a pinch of salt.
- Top the baked flatbread with the tomato mixture. Sprinkle with red pepper flakes (optional). Cut into slices and serve.

# Explore the Middle East

The Middle East is a region located to the northeast of Africa. Asia is to the east and Eastern Europe and Russia are to the north. There are 18 countries that are commonly included in the Middle East, including Saudi Arabia, Iran, Israel, and Lebanon. The Middle East is considered part of the larger Asian continent due to its geographical location and cultural ties to the wider Asian community, though its foods are distinct to themselves, so we chose to highlight them in their own chapter.

We are focusing on the recipes from two Middle Eastern countries:

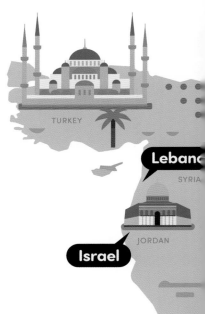

KAZAKHSTAN

UZBEKISTAN

KYRGYSTAN

TURKMENISTAN

TAJIKISTAN

IRAN

AFGHANISTAN

PAKISTAN

AUDI
RABIA

UNITED ARAB
EMIRATES

OMAN

YEMEN

# Israel

Israel is located in the Middle East bordered by the Mediterranean Sea to the west and along the northern shore of the Red Sea. Its neighbors include Egypt, Jordan, Lebanon, Syria, and the Palestinian territories of the West Bank and the Gaza Strip. Like most countries on the Mediterranean Sea, Israel's cuisine is influenced by foods common to the region, such as olives, wheat, chickpeas, fish, tomatoes, eggplant, and zucchini.

בתיאבון
Be'te'avon
(be-te-a-von)
*"Good appetite" in Hebrew*

## YOU'LL COOK:

**Braised Beef Brisket with Root Vegetables and Potato Pancakes (Brisket with Latkes)**

**Fried Meat or Chickpea Patties with Cucumber Yogurt Sauce and Quinoa Salad (Falafel with Tzatziki and Tabbouleh)**

**Roasted Cauliflower with Tahini Sauce, Greens, and Farro Salad (Za'atar Cauliflower Steaks)**

## DID YOU KNOW...

- The lowest point on Earth is the Dead Sea (about 1,414 feet/431 meters below sea level), and it borders Israel, the West Bank, and Jordan. It is hard to swim in the Dead Sea because the water contains so much salt that it makes your body float on the surface.

- Jerusalem was founded in 1010 BCE, but there's evidence of settlements dating back to 4500 BCE. This means people have continuously lived in Jerusalem for more than 6,500 years! As a result of its long history, there are more than 2,000 active archaeological sites in Jerusalem.

- Israel has more museums per capita than any other country in the world.

# Braised Beef Brisket with Root Vegetables and Potato Pancakes
## Brisket with Latkes

Brisket with potato latkes is a traditional main dish served during many Jewish holidays, including Passover and Rosh Hashanah. However, we think this recipe is a delicious meal that can be enjoyed all year-round.

**SERVES**
4

**ALLERGENS**
Dairy-Free,
Gluten-Free Optional,
Vegetarian Optional

**TOTAL PREP & COOK TIME**
2 hours 50 minutes

## What You'll Need

1 yellow onion

3 medium carrots

2 medium parsnips

2 pounds beef brisket

3 teaspoons salt

Pepper

2 tablespoons olive oil, plus more as needed

3 medium potatoes

1 large egg

3 tablespoons all-purpose flour or rice flour

## Vegetarian Option

4 portobello mushrooms or 2 (15-oz) cans green jackfruit

1 pound cremini or button mushrooms

## BRAISIN' MIX

¼ cup tomato paste

¼ cup apple cider vinegar

2 tablespoons Worcestershire sauce

1 tablespoon beef or vegetable bouillon

1 teaspoon dried thyme

1 teaspoon dried rosemary

1 teaspoon dried parsley

1 teaspoon garlic powder

1 bay leaf

### 1. Prep the ingredients ★★

- Preheat the oven to 350°F.
- **Onion**—Peel and thinly slice.
- **Carrots**—Peel, trim the ends, and cut into 1½-inch pieces.
- **Parsnips**—Peel, trim the ends, and cut into 1½-inch pieces.
- **Braisin' Mix**—Combine all the ingredients in a small bowl and mix well.

**Vegetarian option**

- **Portobello mushrooms**—Trim the stems and cut into ¼-inch slices. OR **Green jackfruit**—Drain and cut into big chunks.
- **Cremini or button mushrooms**—Halve large mushrooms and keep small ones whole.

### 2. Cook the meat or mushrooms ★★★

- Season the meat or mushrooms with 1 teaspoon of salt and pepper.
- In a Dutch oven, heat 1 tablespoon of olive oil over medium-high heat.
- Add the seasoned meat or mushrooms and sear until browned, 4 to 5 minutes per side.
- Add the onion, carrots, parsnips, Braisin' Mix, 3½ cups water, 1 teaspoon of salt, and pepper to taste. Stir well to combine.
- Cover, place in the oven, and bake for 1½ to 2 hours for meat (checking every 30 minutes and adding water if it's dry) until tender or 20 to 25 minutes for mushrooms. Remove the bay leaf.

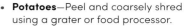

### 3. Prep the latkes ★★

- **Potatoes**—Peel and coarsely shred using a grater or food processor.
- Wrap the shredded potatoes in paper towels and squeeze out as much liquid as possible.
- In a large bowl, combine the shredded potatoes, egg, 3 tablespoons of flour or rice flour, remaining 1 teaspoon of salt, and pepper to taste and mix well.

### 4. Cook the latkes ★★

- In a large nonstick skillet, heat the remaining 1 tablespoon of olive oil over medium-high heat until hot.
- Add 2 tablespoons of the potato mixture to the skillet and flatten it with a fork. Lower the heat to medium.
- Cook until the edges are golden brown, 1 to 2 minutes per side. Transfer the latkes to a plate and cover with foil to keep warm.
- Cook the remaining latkes in batches. Add more oil as needed to keep them from sticking.

### 5. Cut the beef brisket ★★★

- Place the brisket on a cutting board and let rest for 15 minutes.
- Transfer the vegetables to a serving platter and cover with aluminum foil to keep warm.
- Pour the leftover juices through a strainer into a medium serving bowl.
- Cut the brisket against the grain into ½-inch slices.

### 6. Serve your dish ★

- Arrange slices of brisket or the mushrooms on top of the roasted vegetables on the serving platter. Spoon the sauce over the top.
- Serve with the latkes on the side.

# Fried Meat or Chickpea Patties with Cucumber Yogurt Sauce and Quinoa Salad

## Falafel with Tzatziki and Tabbouleh

**SERVES**
4

**ALLERGENS**
Nut-Free, Gluten-Free, Vegetarian Optional

**TOTAL PREP & COOK TIME**
40 minutes

This is a Middle Eastern dish traditionally made with chickpeas, deep-fried, and served in a pita, garnished with various toppings. In our twist, we sauté lean ground meat with fresh herbs and traditional Mediterranean spices, though we offer the classic chickpea option as well.

## What You'll Need

1 cucumber

1 cup cherry tomatoes

4 scallions

1 lemon

1½ pounds ground turkey

1 large egg

2 teaspoons salt, plus more as needed

Pepper

½ cup quinoa

¼ cup plus 1 tablespoon olive oil

2 cups arugula

½ cup plain Greek yogurt

4 pita breads or gluten-free pita

## Vegetarian Option

2 (15-oz) cans chickpeas

1 small onion

12 sprigs parsley

3 tablespoons all-purpose flour or chickpea flour

2 tablespoons sesame seeds (optional)

## FA-LA-LA-FEL SPICE MIX

1 tablespoon ground cumin

2 teaspoons ground coriander

2 teaspoons granulated garlic

1 teaspoon ground sumac

½ teaspoon ground cinnamon

## TASTY TABOULEH MIX

1 tablespoon dried parsley

1 teaspoon granulated garlic

## 1. Prep the ingredients ★★

- **Cucumber**—Trim the ends. Cut into small cubes.
- **Cherry tomatoes**—Cut in half.
- **Scallions**—Trim the ends. Thinly slice. Use half in step 2 and half in step 4.
- **Lemon**—Halve and juice.
- **Fa-la-la-fel Spice Mix**—Combine all the ingredients in a small bowl and mix well.
- **Tasty Tabouleh Mix**—Combine all the ingredients in a small bowl and mix well.

### Vegetarian option

- **Chickpeas**—Drain and rinse.
- **Onion**—Peel and chop.
- **Parsley**—Trim and roughly chop.
- In a food processor, combine the chickpeas, onion, parsley, 3 tablespoons of flour or chickpea flour, and sesame seeds (optional) and process until blended but not pureed.

## 2. Form the falafel ★

- In a large bowl, combine the ground turkey or chickpea mixture, egg, Fa-la-la-fel Spice Mix, half the scallions, 1 teaspoon of salt, and pepper to taste. Stir together until combined.
- Form the mixture into oval shapes about 2 inches in diameter at the widest part.
- Place them on a baking sheet and let rest in the fridge while you prepare the tabouleh.

## 3. Cook the quinoa ★★

- In a medium pot over high heat, combine the quinoa, 1 cup water, and a pinch of salt and bring to a boil.
- Cover, lower the heat to a simmer, and cook until tender, 15 to 20 minutes. Remove from the heat and let cool.

Continued...

# Fried Meat or Chickpea Patties with Cucumber Yogurt Sauce and Quinoa Salad

## Falafel with Tzatziki and Tabbouleh

  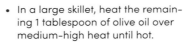 

**4. Make the tabbouleh** ★

- In a serving bowl, combine the Tasty Tabouleh Mix, 2 teaspoons of lemon juice, ¼ cup of olive oil, ½ teaspoon of salt, and pepper to taste. Whisk well to emulsify.
- Add the cooked quinoa, tomatoes, half the cucumber, the remaining scallions, and arugula and toss well to combine.

**5. Cook the falafel and make the sauce** ★★★

- In a large skillet, heat the remaining 1 tablespoon of olive oil over medium-high heat until hot.
- Add the falafel in one layer, being careful not to overcrowd. (You may need to cook them in batches.)
- Brown each side until cooked through, about 2 minutes per side. Transfer them to a plate lined with paper towels.
- In a small bowl, combine the yogurt, 1 teaspoon of lemon juice, remaining cucumber, remaining ½ teaspoon of salt, and pepper to taste. Mix well to combine.

**6. Serve your dish** ★

- Toast the pita and open them to form pockets.
- Add the falafel and top with dollops of yogurt sauce. Serve with the tabouleh salad on the side.

## DID YOU KNOW...

Israel has the highest number of museums per capita in the world. With over 200 museums scattered throughout the country, Israel offers a diverse range of cultural, historical, and art exhibitions.

# Roasted Cauliflower with Tahini Sauce, Greens, and Farro Salad
## Za'atar Cauliflower Steaks

**SERVES**
4

**ALLERGENS**
Dairy-Free Optional,
Vegetarian

**TOTAL PREP & COOK TIME**
45 minutes

Lighten up your next meal with Middle Eastern and Meatless Monday–inspired cauliflower "steaks." These satisfying thick-cut slices of cauliflower are rubbed with za'atar (a unique and aromatic spice blend that includes herbs, ground sumac, and sesame seeds) and then roasted until tender.

### What You'll Need

1 Bosc pear or 1 green apple, or 1 cup pomegranate seeds

1 lemon

1 bunch Swiss chard

3 scallions

2 heads cauliflower

2 teaspoons salt, plus more as needed

Pepper

2 tablespoons plus 1 teaspoon olive oil

3 tablespoons pine nuts (optional)

¼ cup plain Greek yogurt or plant-based yogurt

### FEISTY FARRO MIX

½ cup farro

1 tablespoon dried parsley

### ZA'ATAR SPICE MIX

1 teaspoon dried thyme

½ teaspoon dried marjoram

½ teaspoon dried oregano

¼ teaspoon ground sumac

¼ teaspoon sesame seeds

### TANGY TAHINI MIX

2 tablespoons tahini

1 teaspoon dried parsley

1 teaspoon granulated garlic

1. **Prep the ingredients** ⭐⭐
- Preheat the oven to 400°F.
- **Pear or apple**—Core and dice.
- **Lemon**—Halve and juice.
- **Swiss chard**—Trim the ends. Separate and thinly slice the stalks and roughly chop the leaves.
- **Scallions**—Trim the root and ends. Thinly slice the white parts.
- **Cauliflower**—Cut the head vertically into 1½-inch slices (you should get at least 3 slices per head). Note: Don't worry if you end up with florets—they'll still delicious!
- **Feisty Farro Mix**—Combine all the ingredients in a small bowl and mix well.
- **Za'atar Spice Mix**—Combine all the ingredients in a small bowl and mix well.
- **Tangy Tahini Mix**—Combine all the ingredients in a small bowl and mix well.

2. **Cook the farro and roast the cauliflower** ⭐⭐
- In a saucepan, combine the Feisty Farro Mix, a pinch of salt, and 1 cup water and bring to a boil over medium-high heat.
- Lower the heat to a simmer, cover, and cook until tender, 20 to 25 minutes. Let cool.
- On a baking sheet, combine 1 tablespoon of lemon juice, Za'atar Spice Mix, 1 teaspoon of salt, and pepper to taste.
- Place the cauliflower steaks on the baking sheet and rub both sides with the mixture.
- Place the baking sheet on the middle rack of the oven and roast, flipping them halfway through, until golden brown and tender, 20 to 25 minutes total.

3. **Sauté the Swiss chard** ⭐⭐
- In a large skillet, heat 1 teaspoon of olive oil over medium-high heat until hot.
- Add the Swiss chard and sauté until tender, 3 to 4 minutes. Add salt and pepper to taste.

4. **Make the farro salad** ⭐
- In a medium bowl, whisk together the remaining 2 tablespoons of olive oil, 1 tablespoon of lemon juice, ½ teaspoon of salt, and pepper to taste.
- Add the cooled cooked farro; pear, apple, or pomegranate; Swiss chard; scallions; and pine nuts (optional) and toss until combined. Taste for seasoning.

5. **Make the tahini sauce** ⭐
- In a bowl, combine the Tangy Tahini Mix, 1 tablespoon of lemon juice, ¼ cup of yogurt, 1 tablespoon water, remaining ½ teaspoon of salt, and pepper to taste and whisk well. (Note: Add water, a little at a time, to achieve the desired consistency.)

6. **Serve your dish** ⭐
- Spoon some of the farro salad onto each plate and top with a cauliflower steak and some Swiss chard. Spoon a dollop of tahini sauce over the top.

# Lebanon

Despite being the third-smallest country in the Middle East, Lebanon boasts over 7,000 years of history. It is situated on the Mediterranean Sea and bordered by Syria to the west and north and Israel to the south.

بالصحة
Sahtayn
(SAHH-tain)
*"To your health!" in Lebanese*

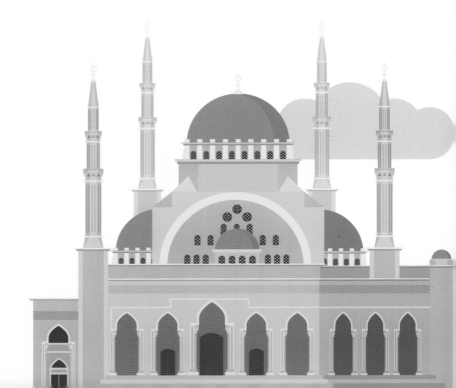

**YOU'LL COOK:**

**Spiced Sliced Beef or Mushrooms with Tahini Sauce and Pita (Shawarma ma' Tarator)**

**Meatballs with Sumac Yogurt Sauce, Grilled Vegetables, and Orzo (Kafta)**

**Ground Beef, Lamb, or Vegetable-Stuffed Zucchini "Canoes" (Kousa Mahshi)**

**DID YOU KNOW...**

• Lebanon has the most religiously diverse society in the Middle East. Its unique cultural history comes from the many foreign rulers who occupied the country, including the Roman Empire, Ottoman Empire, France, and Israel. These foreign powers helped shape the Lebanese cuisine as we know it today.

• It is the only Middle Eastern country that does not have a desert.

• Lebanon is the oldest country name in the world, remaining unchanged for over 4,000 years!

# Spiced Sliced Beef or Mushrooms with Tahini Sauce and Pita
## Shawarma ma' Tarator

Shawarma is a Middle Eastern method of slowly pit-roasting meat on a rotating skewer. Originally brought to Lebanon from Ottoman Turkey and made with lamb, shawarma today is also made with chicken, turkey, beef, and veal. It is the king of street foods in Lebanon and is typically topped with pickled onions, cucumbers, tahini, parsley, and tomatoes.

**SERVES**
4

**ALLERGENS**
Dairy-Free, Nut-Free, Gluten-Free Optional, Vegetarian Optional

**TOTAL PREP & COOK TIME**
20 minutes + at least 30 minutes to marinate

### What You'll Need

1½ pounds sirloin steak or boneless skinless chicken breasts

1 medium onion

¼ cup apple cider vinegar

¼ cup olive oil, plus more as needed

2½ teaspoons salt

Pepper

1 cucumber

2 cups cherry tomatoes

½ lemon

4 pita breads or gluten-free pita

### Vegetarian Option

6 large portobello mushrooms

### SHAWARMA AROMATIC SPICE MIX

2 teaspoons granulated garlic

1 teaspoon ground cumin

1 teaspoon paprika

½ teaspoon ground cloves

½ teaspoon dried oregano

½ teaspoon ground cardamon

½ teaspoon ground cinnamon

¼ teaspoon cayenne pepper

¼ teaspoon ground ginger

### TANGY TAHINI MIX

2 tablespoons tahini

1 teaspoon garlic powder

1 teaspoon dried parsley

1. **Marinate the beef or chicken ★★ (at least 30 minutes at room temperature)**

- **Beef or chicken**—Cut into ⅛-inch slices.
- **Onion**—Peel and dice.
- **Shawarma Aromatic Spice Mix**—Combine all the ingredients in a small bowl and mix well.
- In a large bowl, combine the sliced beef or chicken, onion, Shawarma Aromatic Spice Mix, ¼ cup of apple cider vinegar, ¼ cup of olive oil, 1½ teaspoons of salt, and pepper to taste. Toss well and cover.
- Marinate at room temperature for 30 minutes or for 2 hours and up to overnight in the refrigerator.

2. **Prep the vegetables ★★**

- **Cucumber**—Trim the ends. Cut into ⅛-inch slices.
- **Cherry tomatoes**—Cut in half.
- **Lemon**—Juice.

**Vegetarian option**

- **Portobello mushrooms**—Remove the stems and discard. Cut into ¼-inch slices.
- In a large bowl, combine the sliced mushrooms, Shawarma Aromatic Spice Mix, 3 tablespoons of olive oil, 1 teaspoon of salt, and pepper to taste. Toss well to thoroughly coat.

3. **Make the tahini sauce ★**

- In a jar with a lid, combine all the Tangy Tahini Mix ingredients, 2 tablespoons lemon juice, 5 tablespoons water, remaining 1 teaspoon of salt, and pepper to taste and shake until well blended.

4. **Broil the meat or portobello mushrooms ★★★**

- Adjust the top oven rack to 6 inches below the broiler. Preheat the broiler to high.
- Line a baking sheet with aluminum foil and lightly grease with oil.
- Spread out the marinated steak, chicken, or mushrooms on the baking sheet.
- Broil until the meat or mushrooms are slightly brown and cooked through, 5 to 6 minutes. Be sure to keep an eye on the broiler the entire time so they don't burn.

5. **Serve your dish ★**

- Cut the pita bread in half and gently pry open to create a pocket. Warm the pita bread in the microwave until pliable, 10 to 15 seconds.
- Fill each pita with 4 or 5 slices of meat or mushrooms, sliced cucumber, and tomatoes and top with the tahini sauce.

# Meatballs with Sumac Yogurt Sauce, Grilled Vegetables, and Orzo
## Kafta

Every country has its own version of meatballs. In Lebanon, they call them kafta and they are made with a mixture of ground lamb and beef along with spices and herbs. Serve them with a yogurt sauce that has a hint of sumac—a spice with a slight lemon-lime tang—and it will transport you to the street vendors of Beirut and Tripoli.

 **SERVES**
4

 **ALLERGENS**
Nut-Free,
Gluten-Free Optional,
Vegetarian Optional

 **TOTAL PREP & COOK TIME**
40 minutes

## What You'll Need

1 small red onion

1 red bell pepper

1 large zucchini

1 small eggplant

4½ teaspoons salt, plus more as needed

1 cup orzo or gluten-free orzo

2 tablespoons butter

2 tablespoons olive oil, plus more as needed

1 pound ground beef

8 ounces ground lamb

1 egg

¾ cup panko, breadcrumbs, or gluten-free panko

1 teaspoon sugar

Pepper

½ cup plain Greek yogurt

### Vegetarian Option

1 (15-oz) can black beans

1 (15-oz) can lentils

### K'KAFTA MIX

2 teaspoons granulated garlic

2 teaspoons ground cumin

1½ teaspoons dried parsley

1½ teaspoons dried mint

1½ teaspoons dried cilantro

1 teaspoon ground coriander

½ teaspoon ground cloves

½ teaspoon ground cinnamon

½ teaspoon ground allspice

½ teaspoon ground cardamon

### GARLICKY SUMAC MIX

2 teaspoons granulated garlic

2 teaspoons dried parsley

1 teaspoon ground sumac

1. **Prep the ingredients** ★★

- **Red onion**—Peel and cut in half. Finely dice half for step 3. Cut the remaining half into ⅛-inch slices for step 4.
- **Red bell pepper**—Cut in half, discard the stem and seeds, and cut into ½-inch slices.
- **Zucchini**—Trim the ends and cut into ¼-inch slices.
- **Eggplant**—Trim the ends and cut into ¼-inch slices.
- **K'kafta Mix**—Combine all the ingredients in a small bowl and mix well.
- **Garlicky Sumac Mix**—Combine all the ingredients in a small bowl and mix well.

**Vegetarian option**

- **Black beans and lentils**—Rinse and drain. In a large bowl, combine the black beans and lentils and mash well with a potato masher.

2. **Cook the orzo** ★★

- Bring a large pot of salted water to a boil. Add the orzo and cook until al dente, 8 to 10 minutes.
- Drain in a colander and transfer to a serving bowl.
- Add 2 tablespoons of butter and stir to coat. Using a fork, fluff the orzo.

3. **Prep the kafta** ★

- Lightly grease 2 baking sheets with olive oil.
- In a large bowl, combine the ground beef and lamb until well mixed.
- Combine the meat or bean and lentil mixture, diced red onion, egg, K'kafta Mix, ¾ cup of panko or breadcrumbs, 1 teaspoon of sugar, and 2 teaspoons of salt.
- Using clean hands, gently fold the meat or bean mixture together. Form the mixture into 1-inch balls (you can use a small ice cream scoop!). Place them on one of the baking sheets, making sure they don't touch.

Continued...

# Meatballs with Sumac Yogurt Sauce, Grilled Vegetables, and Orzo
## Kafta

### 4. Prep the vegetables ★

- In a large bowl, combine the sliced red onion, red bell pepper, zucchini, eggplant, 2 tablespoon of olive oil, 2 teaspoons of salt, and pepper to taste.
- Spread the vegetables out evenly on the second baking sheet.

### 5. Broil the kafta, then broil the vegetables ★★★

- Adjust the top oven rack to 6 inches below the broiler. Preheat the broiler to high.
- Place the baking sheet with the meatballs on the top rack and broil until golden brown, 6 to 7 minutes.
- Flip the meatballs and cook for another 5 to 6 minutes. Be sure to keep an eye on the broiler the entire time so they don't burn! Keep warm until ready to serve.
- Place the baking sheet with the vegetables on the top rack and broil until slightly charred, 5 to 6 minutes. Keep warm until ready to serve.

### 6. Prep the yogurt sauce and serve your dish ★

- In a bowl, combine the yogurt, Garlicky Sumac Mix, remaining ½ teaspoon of salt, and pepper to taste and stir until well mixed.
- Place 4 or 5 meatballs on each individual plate along with some grilled vegetables and buttered orzo. Top the meatballs with a few dollops of the yogurt sauce.

## DID YOU KNOW...

Lebanon is home to the world's oldest continuously inhabited city. The city of Byblos in Lebanon has a history that dates back over 7,000 years.

# Ground Beef, Lamb, or Vegetable-Stuffed Zucchini "Canoes"

## Kousa Mahshi

This dish, called kousa mahshi in Lebanon, is popular in the summer months when zucchini is at its prime. The traditional way to make it is to hollow out zucchini halves, which we do here, and stuff it with a spiced meat filling.

 **SERVES**
4

 **ALLERGENS**
Dairy-Free, Nut-Free, Gluten-Free, Vegetarian Optional

 **TOTAL PREP & COOK TIME**
1 hour

### What You'll Need

6 medium zucchini

1 medium onion

1 cup basmati or other long-grain rice

3 teaspoons salt, plus more as needed

1 tablespoon olive oil

12 ounces ground beef or lamb

Pepper

1 (28-oz) can crushed tomatoes

¼ teaspoon sugar

### Vegetarian Option

1 (15-oz) can chickpeas

1 carrot

¼ cup crushed tomatoes

### MMMM MAHSHI SPICE MIX

1 tablespoon dried parsley

1 tablespoon dried mint

2 teaspoons granulated garlic

2 teaspoons ground allspice

2 teaspoons ground cumin

1 teaspoon ground coriander

½ teaspoon lemon peel granules

### SHHH ONION MIX

1 teaspoon onion powder

1 teaspoon vegetable bouillon

¼ teaspoon sugar

### 1. Prep the ingredients ★★

- Preheat the oven to 400°F.
- **Zucchini**—Trim the ends and halve lengthwise. Using a spoon or a melon baller, gently scoop out the seeds to create "canoes." Roughly chop the scooped-out zucchini flesh and reserve for step 3.
- **Onion**—Peel and dice.
- **Mmmm Mahshi Spice Mix**—Combine all the ingredients in a small bowl and mix well.
- **Shhh Onion Mix**—Combine all the ingredients in a small bowl and mix well.

**Vegetarian option**

- **Chickpeas**—Drain and rinse in a colander.
- **Carrot**—Peel and dice.
- In a bowl, combine the chickpeas, carrot, and crushed tomatoes.

### 2. Cook the rice ★★

- Rinse the rice in a colander to remove excess starch.
- In a small pot over medium-high heat, combine the rice, a pinch of salt, and 1½ cups water and bring to a boil.
- Lower the heat, cover, and simmer until the liquid has been absorbed and the rice is tender, about 15 minutes.
- Remove from the heat, fluff the cooked rice with a fork, and keep warm until ready to serve.
- Use 1 cup in step 5. Use the remaining rice in step 6.

### 3. Sauté the filling ★★

- In a large skillet, heat 1 tablespoon of olive oil over medium-high heat until hot.
- Add the onion and Mmmm Mahshi Spice Mix and sauté until tender, about 3 minutes.
- Add the meat or chickpea mixture, 1 teaspoon of salt, and pepper to taste. Sauté, using a spoon to crumble the meat, until cooked through, about 5 minutes.

### 4. Prep the stuffing and make the tomato sauce ★

- In a large bowl, combine the meat or vegetable mixture, chopped zucchini, 1 cup of the cooked rice, 1 teaspoon of salt, and pepper to taste and mix well.
- In a separate medium bowl, combine the crushed tomatoes, Shhh Onion Mix, remaining 1 teaspoon of salt, ¼ teaspoon of sugar, and 1 cup water and mix well.

### 5. Stuff and bake the zucchini "canoes" ★★

- Using two 9-by-13-inch baking dishes, divide the tomato sauce equally between the baking dishes and spread it out evenly.
- Place the zucchini "canoes" with the open side up on the tomato sauce. Stuff each zucchini "canoe" with 3 to 4 tablespoons of the filling.
- Bake until the zucchini "canoes" are tender, 25 to 30 minutes.

### 6. Serve your dish ★

- Place three zucchini "canoes" on each individual plate, top with some of the tomato sauce in the baking dish, and serve with the remaining rice on the side.

# Explore
# the Americas

The Americas are made up of the continents of North America and South America. Located in the Western Hemisphere, North America is the third largest and South America is the fourth largest continents in the world. They are both bordered by the Atlantic Ocean and the Pacific Ocean.

Canada is the largest country in land mass while the United States is the most populous country in North America. Brazil is the largest and most populous country in South America.

The recipes featured in this chapter come from:

CANADA

USA

Mexico

Peru

Brazil

# Brazil

As the largest country in South America and the fifth largest in the world, Brazil has one of the most diverse food cultures thanks to the different immigrants who arrived from countries like Portugal, Germany, Japan, Italy, Lebanon, and the continent of Africa and made Brazil their home.

Bom apetite
(bom ap-e-chi-chi)
*"Enjoy your meal!" in Brazilian Portuguese*

## YOU'LL COOK:

**Meat or Vegetable Stew with Rice and Collard Greens (Feijoada)**

**Shrimp and Coconut Milk Stew with Peppers, Spinach, and Rice (Moqueca)**

**Brazilian Savory Meat Pastries with Tomato and Watermelon Salad (Pastéis)**

- The Amazon is the largest remaining rainforest in the world, spanning just over two million miles (twice the size of India!). Nearly 60 percent of the Amazon rainforest is contained within Brazil.

- Brazil is the only country in South America that speaks Portuguese because immigrants from Portugal colonized the country back in the 16th century, bringing with them their language as well as their food traditions. The other South American countries mainly speak Spanish.

- Brazil is the largest Portuguese-speaking country in the world.

# Meat or Vegetable Stew with Rice and Collard Greens
## Feijoada

The national dish of Brazil, feijoada is a comforting peasant stew of black beans and meat. Its name comes from "feijao," the Portuguese word for beans. This dish was influenced by two early settlers in Brazil: Portuguese colonists and African slaves.

**SERVES**
4

**ALLERGENS**
Dairy-Free, Nut-Free, Gluten-Free, Vegetarian Optional

**TOTAL PREP & COOK TIME**
1 hour 10 minutes

### What You'll Need

1 medium onion

1 orange

10 ounces collard greens or kale

4 ounces bacon

1 pound chorizo or chicken sausage

1½ pounds pork ribs or chicken thighs

2 (15-oz) cans black beans

1½ cups basmati or other long-grain rice

½ teaspoon salt, plus more as needed

4 teaspoons olive oil

Pepper

Hot sauce (optional)

### Vegetarian Option

1 butternut squash or 2 sweet potatoes

2 red bell peppers

6 ounces okra

1 tablespoon olive oil

### BAYISH GARLIC MIX

2 teaspoons granulated garlic

2 teaspoons chicken or vegetable bouillon

2 bay leaves

### FAROFA MIX

¼ cup cassava meal

1 teaspoon granulated garlic

1. **Prep the ingredients** ★

- **Onion**—Peel and dice.
- **Orange**—Using a sharp knife, trim away the rind. Cut into ¼-inch slices
- **Collard greens or kale**—Separate the center ribs from the leaves and discard them. Cut the leaves into ⅛-inch slices.
- **Bacon**—Cut into ¼-inch slices.
- **Sausages**—Cut into ½-inch pieces.
- **Pork ribs**—Cut into individual ribs. OR **Chicken thighs**—Cut into quarters.
- **Bayish Garlic Mix**—Combine all the ingredients in a small bowl and mix well.
- **Farofa Mix**—Combine all the ingredients in a small bowl and mix well.

**Vegetarian option**

- **Butternut squash**—Peel and cut into 1-inch pieces.
- **Bell peppers**—Cut in half, discard the stem and seeds, and dice.
- **Okra**—Trim the ends. Cut into ½-inch pieces.

2. **Cook the feijoada** ★★★

- In a Dutch oven or heavy-bottomed pot with a lid, cook the bacon over medium heat until the fat renders, about 3 minutes (or heat 1 tablespoon oil for vegetarian optional).
- Add the onion and sauté until tender, about 2 minutes.
- Add the sausages, pork ribs or chicken thighs OR the butternut squash, bell peppers, and okra and the Bayish Garlic Mix and brown the meat or sauté the vegetables for 1 to 2 minutes.
- Add the black beans and 2 cups water and bring to a boil. Lower the heat and simmer until the meat falls off the bone or the vegetables are tender, 1 hour for ribs, 30 minutes for chicken, or 20 minutes for vegetables. Remove the bay leaves.

3. **Cook the rice (while the feijoada is simmering)** ★★

- Rinse the rice in a colander to remove excess starch.
- In a small pot, combine the rice, a pinch of salt, and 2¼ cups water. Bring to a boil over medium-high heat.
- Lower the heat, cover, and simmer until the liquid has been absorbed and the rice is tender, about 15 minutes.
- Remove from the heat, fluff the cooked rice with a fork, and keep warm until ready to serve.

Continued…

# Meat or Vegetable Stew with Rice and Collard Greens
## Feijoada

**4. Prep the farofa ★★
(while the feijoada is simmering)**

- In a large skillet, heat 1 teaspoon of olive oil over medium-high heat.
- Add the Farofa Mix and stir continuously until toasted, 3 to 5 minutes.
- Add salt and pepper to taste. Transfer to a small serving bowl.

**5. Sauté the collard greens ★★
or kale (5 minutes before the
feijoada is ready)**

- In the same skillet as the farofa, heat the remaining 3 teaspoons of olive oil over medium-high heat.
- Add the collard greens or kale, ½ teaspoon of salt, and pepper to taste.
- Sauté until wilted, 2 to 3 minutes.

**6. Serve your dish ★**

- Spoon the rice onto individual plates and add the feijoada and greens.
- Garnish with the farofa and orange slices. Top with hot sauce (optional).

## DID YOU KNOW...

The Amazon River flows through Brazil and is the second longest river in the world (the Nile, in Africa, is the longest).

# Shrimp and Coconut Milk Stew with Peppers, Spinach, and Rice
## Moqueca

 **SERVES**
4

 **ALLERGENS**
Dairy-Free,
Nut-Free, Gluten-Free,
Vegetarian Optional

 **TOTAL PREP & COOK TIME**
30 minutes

Moqueca is the dish that most represents Brazilian cuisine today, as it is a mashup of Native Indian, African, and Portuguese influences. The dish is also called muqueca or mu'kaka from an Angolan dialect, or pokeka in the Tupi Native dialect. Big and bold, this shrimp and coconut milk stew is simple to make but bursting with flavor!

## What You'll Need

1½ pounds medium shrimp

1 onion

1 red bell pepper

1 lemon

8 ounces fresh spinach

1½ cups basmati or other long-grain rice

1 teaspoon salt, plus more as needed

1 tablespoon olive oil

1 (15-oz) can diced tomatoes

1 (15-oz) can coconut milk

2 tablespoons apple cider vinegar

1 teaspoon sugar

### Vegetarian Option

2 (15-oz) cans chickpeas

1 (16-oz) package firm tofu

### SAMBANDO MOQUECA

2 teaspoons granulated garlic

2 teaspoons dried cilantro

2 teaspoons dried parsley

¼ teaspoon lemon peel granules

### 1. Prep the ingredients ★

- **Shrimp**—Remove the shell and tail.
- **Onion**—Peel and cut into ⅛-inch slices.
- **Bell pepper**—Cut in half, discard the stem and seeds, and dice.
- **Lemon**—Cut in half and juice.
- **Spinach**—Rinse and roughly chop.
- **Sambando Moqueca**—Combine all the ingredients in a small bowl and mix well.

#### Vegetarian option

- **Chickpeas**—Drain and rinse using a colander.
- **Tofu**—Drain. Use paper towels to press out the liquid from the tofu. Cut into ½-inch cubes.

### 2. Cook the rice ★★★

- Rinse the rice in a colander to remove excess starch.
- In a small pot, combine the rice, a pinch of salt, and 2¼ cups water. Bring to a boil over medium-high heat.
- Lower the heat, cover, and simmer until the liquid has been absorbed and the rice is tender, about 15 minutes.
- Remove from the heat, fluff the cooked rice with a fork, and keep warm until ready to serve.

### 3. Cook the vegetables ★★★

- In a Dutch oven or heavy-bottomed pot, heat 1 tablespoon of olive oil over medium heat until hot.
- Add the onion, red bell pepper, and Sambando Moqueca and sauté until tender, about 3 minutes.
- Add the diced tomatoes, lemon juice, coconut milk, 2 tablespoons of apple cider vinegar, 1 teaspoon of salt, and 1 teaspoon of sugar and simmer for 3 to 5 minutes.
- Add the shrimp or chickpeas and tofu, and the spinach and cook until cooked through (the shrimp will curl up and turn light pink), 2 to 3 minutes.
- If the moqueca starts getting thick and dry, stir in 2 tablespoons water.

### 4. Serve your dish ★

- Spoon rice into individual bowls and top with the moqueca.

# Brazilian Savory Meat Pastries with Tomato and Watermelon Salad
## Pastéis

Most countries have a version of a savory pastry, and in Brazil they are called pastéis. They are normally deep-fried, but our healthier version is baked, using flaky puff pastry dough. Making pastéis is fun and easy—roll out the dough, fill it with ground beef or chicken, seal, and bake.

 **SERVES**
4

 **ALLERGENS**
Dairy-Free, Nut-Free,
Gluten-Free Optional,
Vegetarian Optional

 **TOTAL PREP & COOK TIME**
40 minutes

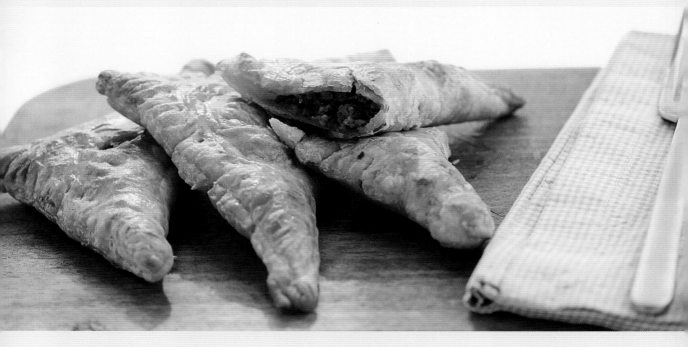

### What You'll Need

1 medium yellow onion

1 cup cherry tomatoes

8 ounces watermelon

1 large egg

Lime (optional)

1 tablespoon plus
2 teaspoons olive oil

1 pound ground beef or chicken

1 tablespoon tomato paste

1¼ teaspoons salt

All-purpose flour or gluten-free flour,
for dusting

2 sheets puff pastry or gluten-free
puff pastry

1 tablespoon balsamic vinegar

½ teaspoon honey (optional)

Pepper

### Vegetarian Option

1 pound button mushrooms

4 kale leaves

### E2E CHILI MIX

½ teaspoon ground cumin

½ teaspoon chili powder

½ teaspoon paprika

½ teaspoon granulated garlic

½ teaspoon ground cinnamon

¼ teaspoon sugar

### 1. Prep the ingredients ★★

- Preheat the oven to 425°F. Line a baking sheet with parchment paper.
- **Onion**—Peel and dice.
- **Cherry tomatoes**—Cut in half.
- **Watermelon**—Cut off the rind and into ¼-inch cubes.
- **Egg**—Whisk together the egg with 1 tablespoon water to make an egg wash.
- **Lime (optional)**—Juice half for step 2 and cut the remaining half into quarters for garnish.
- **e2e Chili Mix**—Combine all the ingredients in a small bowl and mix well.

#### Vegetarian option

- **Mushrooms**—Rinse and thinly slice.
- **Kale**—Separate the center ribs from the leaves and discard them. Thinly slice the leaves.

### 2. Cook the meat filling ★★

- In a large skillet, heat 1 tablespoon of olive oil over medium-high heat until hot.
- Add the onion and sauté until tender, 1 to 2 minutes.
- Add the ground beef or chicken or the mushrooms and kale, and the e2e Chili Mix and cook, using a fork or wooden spoon to break up the meat, until browned, about 3 minutes.
- Add 2 tablespoons water, the tomato paste, 1 teaspoon of salt, and ½ teaspoon of lime juice (optional) and stir until combined. Let simmer for 3 to 5 minutes.

### 3. Assemble and bake the pastéis ★

- Lightly dust a clean surface with flour or gluten-free flour.
- Using a rolling pin, roll out each sheet of puff pastry into a 12-by-12-inch square. Cut each sheet into four 6-by-6-inch squares.
- Place 3 tablespoons of the meat or mushroom mixture in the middle of each square. Fold the puff pastry in half, making it into a triangle. Use a fork to crimp and seal the edges.
- Place each pastéis on the prepared baking sheet.
- Brush the tops with the egg wash. Cut small slits in the center of each pastéis.
- Bake for 5 minutes, flip over, and bake for another 5 minutes, until golden brown.

### 4. Assemble the salad ★

- In a large bowl, whisk together the balsamic vinegar, remaining 2 teaspoons of olive oil, ½ teaspoon of honey (optional), remaining ¼ teaspoon of salt, and pepper to taste.
- Add the watermelon and tomatoes and gently toss to combine.

### 5. Serve your dish ★

- Place two warm pastéis on each plate and serve with the tomato and watermelon salad.

# Peru

Peru is on the west side of South America and is bordered by Ecuador to the north, Chile to the south, Bolivia to the southeast, and Brazil to the east. It has one of the longest histories of civilization of any country, dating back to the 4th millennia BCE, and was home to several ancient cultures, including the oldest ancient civilization in the Americas, the Norte Chico civilization. Peru is most commonly known for its 15th-century Inca citadel, Machu Picchu.

¡Provecho!
(pro-BAY-cho)
*"Good appetite!" in Spanish*

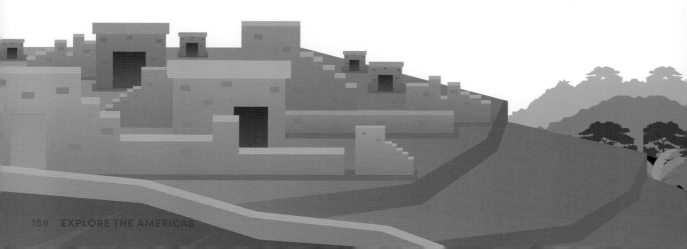

**YOU'LL COOK:**

**Peruvian Stir-Fried Beef with Rice (Lomo Saltado)**

**Peruvian Stuffed Potatoes with Quinoa Salad (Papa Rellena)**

**Roasted Chicken with Green Chile Sauce, Roasted Potatoes, and Green Beans (Pollo a la Brasa con Aji Verde)**

**DID YOU KNOW...**

- Potatoes originated in Peru and there are more than 4,000 varieties grown in the country!

- The Amazon River starts in Peru.

- Sixty percent of Peru is covered by the Amazon rainforest.

# Peruvian Stir-Fried Beef with Rice
## Lomo Saltado

This dish is a famous Peruvian stir-fry that originated from Chinese immigrants. This kind of fusion cuisine is known as chifa, which comes from the Chinese words "chi fan," meaning "to eat." Chifa uses Chinese techniques and ingredients and combines them with Peruvian ingredients. "Lomo saltado" means "jumped loin" and is so named because when beef is stir-fried over a high flame it "jumps" while it cooks.

 **SERVES**
4

 **ALLERGENS**
Dairy-Free, Nut-Free

 **TOTAL PREP & COOK TIME**
45 minutes

### What You'll Need

2 pounds beef sirloin or chicken tenderloin

1 teaspoon salt, plus more if needed

1 teaspoon pepper

1 medium red onion

2 plum tomatoes

1 red bell pepper

3 russet potatoes

1½ cups jasmine rice

Vegetable oil

### LOMITO SALTITO SAUCE

3 tablespoons soy sauce

3 tablespoons red wine vinegar

1 tablespoon oyster sauce

1 tablespoon dried cilantro

1 teaspoon aji amarillo paste

1 teaspoon garlic powder

### 1. Prep the ingredients ★★★

- **Steak or chicken**—Cut into ¼-inch slices. Season with 1 teaspoon of salt and the pepper and set aside (Note: For steak, cut against the grain.)
- **Red onion**—Peel and cut into ¼-inch slices.
- **Tomatoes**—Cut in half, remove the seeds, and cut into ¼-inch slices.
- **Bell pepper**—Cut in half, discard the stem and seeds, and cut into ¼-inch slices.
- **Potatoes**—Peel and cut into ½-inch sticks (like french fries).
- **Lomito Saltito Sauce**—Combine all the ingredients in a small bowl and mix well.

### 2. Cook the rice ★★

- Rinse the rice in a colander to remove excess starch.
- In a small pot, combine the rice, a pinch of salt, and 2¼ cups water. Bring to a boil over medium-high heat.
- Lower the heat, cover, and simmer until the liquid has been absorbed and the rice is tender, about 15 minutes.
- Remove from the heat, fluff the cooked rice with a fork, and keep warm until ready to serve.

### 3. Cook the potatoes (while the rice is cooking) ★★★

**DEEP FRY**

- In a deep heavy-bottomed pot or deep fryer, heat 1 inch of vegetable oil over medium-high heat until hot (340°F). Pat dry the potatoes with paper towels. Carefully add the potato sticks and cook until crispy and golden, 5 to 7 minutes. Drain well on paper towels.

**BAKE**

- Preheat the oven to 375°F. Toss the potatoes with oil and spread them in a single layer on a baking sheet.
- Bake for 20 minutes. Increase the heat to 450°F and continue baking until crispy, 10 to 15 minutes.

### 4. Cook the stir-fry (while the rice is cooking) ★★★

- In a skillet, heat 2 tablespoons of oil over medium heat until hot. Add the meat and stir-fry until browned, 2 to 3 minutes. Transfer to a plate.
- In the same skillet, combine the onion and bell peppers and stir-fry until tender, 3 to 5 minutes.
- Add the meat, Lomito Saltito Sauce, and tomatoes and stir-fry over medium-high heat until coated with sauce, about 1 minute. Do not overcook or the tomatoes will make the stir-fry watery.

### 5. Serve your dish ★

- Top the stir-fried meat with the fried potatoes and serve with a side of rice.

# Peruvian Stuffed Potatoes with Quinoa Salad
## Papa Rellena

Who doesn't like fried stuffed mashed potatoes? There are many countries with their own versions of stuffed mashed potatoes: croquetas from Spain, croquettes from France, aloo tikki from India, korokke from Japan, and crocchette from Italy. Peru's version is called papa rellena and it's a great comfort food that kids of all ages will love.

**SERVES**
4

**ALLERGENS**
Nut-Free

**TOTAL PREP & COOK TIME**
45 minutes

## What You'll Need

1 medium onion

3 tomatoes

½ cup pitted black olives

3 pounds yellow potatoes (about 6 medium potatoes)

2 eggs

¼ cup whole milk

2 tablespoons butter

2¼ teaspoons salt, plus more as needed

Pepper

½ cup quinoa

3 tablespoons olive oil

12 ounces ground beef or chicken

¼ cup raisins

1 cup fresh or frozen corn kernels

1 cup frozen fava beans

1 tablespoon red or white wine vinegar

4 ounces queso fresco (optional)

All-purpose flour

Vegetable oil, for frying

### E2E CHILI MIX

½ teaspoon ground cumin

½ teaspoon chili powder

½ teaspoon paprika

½ teaspoon granulated garlic

½ teaspoon ground cinnamon

¼ teaspoon sugar

### 1. Prep the ingredients ★★★

- **Onion**—Peel and dice. Use half in step 4 and half in step 5.
- **Tomatoes**—Cut in half, remove the seeds, and dice. Use half in step 4 and half in step 5.
- **Black olives**—Thinly slice. Use half in step 4 and half in step 5.
- **Potatoes**—Peel and cut into ½-inch pieces. Put them in a pot and cover with salted water.
- **Eggs**—In a saucepan, combine the eggs and enough cold water to cover them. Bring to a boil, turn off the heat, cover, and let sit for 10 minutes. Drain and peel once cool. Cut into quarters.
- **e2e Chili Mix**—Combine all the ingredients in a small bowl and mix well.

### 2. Make the mashed potatoes ★★

- Set the pot of potatoes over medium-high heat and bring to a boil.
- Decrease the heat to a simmer and cook for 10 minutes or until potatoes are soft and tender.
- Drain the potatoes in a colander and return to the pot.
- Add ¼ cup of milk, 2 tablespoons of butter, ¼ teaspoon of salt, and pepper to taste.
- Mash the potatoes using a potato masher until smooth. Add a little water if needed to reach the desired consistency.

### 3. Cook the quinoa ★★

- In a medium pot, combine the quinoa, 1 cup water, and a pinch of salt.
- Bring to a boil over high heat. Cover, lower the heat to a simmer, and cook until tender, 15 to 20 minutes.
- Remove from the heat and let cool.

Continued...

# Peruvian Stuffed Potatoes with Quinoa Salad
## Papa Rellena

### 4. Cook the filling (while the potatoes are cooking) ★★★

- In a large skillet, heat 1 tablespoon of olive oil over medium-high heat until hot.
- Add half the diced onion and sauté until tender, 1 to 2 minutes.
- Add the ground beef or chicken and the e2e Chili Mix and cook, using a fork or wooden spoon to break up the meat, until browned, about 3 minutes.
- Add 2 tablespoons water, half the diced tomatoes, half the sliced olives, ¼ cup of raisins, and 1 teaspoon of salt and stir until combined. Let simmer for 3 to 5 minutes. Transfer to a plate.

### 5. Make the quinoa salad ★

- In the same large skillet, heat 1 tablespoon of olive oil over medium-high heat until hot.
- Add the remaining diced onion and sauté until tender, 1 to 2 minutes.
- Add the corn, fava beans, remaining 1 teaspoon of salt, and pepper to taste. Sauté for 1 to 2 minutes.
- Transfer the corn and fava bean mixture to a bowl, add the cooked quinoa, remaining diced tomatoes, remaining sliced olives, 1 tablespoon of red or white wine vinegar, and remaining 1 tablespoon of olive oil. Mix well and season with salt and pepper to taste.
- Optional: Add crumbled queso fresco.

### 6. Cook the stuffed potatoes and serve ★★

- Shape the mashed potatoes into 8 oval balls. Flatten the potato balls and place some of the meat filling and a quarter of a hard-boiled egg in the center of the flattened potato ball.
- Fold up the potato over the stuffing and reshape into ovals. If it is difficult to seal the stuffing, add some mashed potato to help seal it.
- Repeat with the rest of the mashed potato balls and filling. Coat each stuffed potato with flour.
- In a deep heavy-bottomed pot, heat 2 inches of vegetable oil over medium-high heat until hot (360°F). Carefully add the stuffed potatoes and cook until crispy and golden, 6 to 8 minutes. Drain well on paper towels.
- Serve the stuffed potatoes hot with the quinoa salad on the side.

## DID YOU KNOW...

Peru has the world's deepest canyon. The Colca Canyon, located in southern Peru, reaches a depth of about 3,270 meters (10,730 feet), making it twice as deep as the Grand Canyon in the United States.

# Roasted Chicken with Green Chile Sauce, Roasted Potatoes, and Green Beans
## Pollo a la Brasa con Aji Verde

One of the better-known dishes in Peru, this roasted or rotisserie chicken is packed with influences from the Chinese and Japanese Peruvian communities. The key to this recipe is the intensely flavored green sauce, aji verde, that accompanies the tasty roasted chicken thighs.

**SERVES**
4

**ALLERGENS**
Nut-Free

**TOTAL PREP & COOK TIME**
45 minutes + 2 hours or up to overnight to marinate

## What You'll Need

8 bone-in, skin-on chicken thighs

7 tablespoons olive oil, plus more as needed

1½ pounds multicolor baby potatoes

1 pound green beans

2 garlic cloves

1 lime

1¼ teaspoons salt

Pepper

½ cup mayonnaise

2 tablespoons grated Parmesan cheese

Red pepper flakes (optional)

### BRASA MIX

½ cup soy sauce

2 tablespoons lime juice

1 tablespoon garlic powder

1 tablespoon ground cumin

2 teaspoons paprika

1 teaspoon dried oregano

1 teaspoon aji amarillo paste

### AJI VERDE MIX

3 tablespoons dried cilantro

½ teaspoon granulated garlic

¼ teaspoon red pepper flakes

### 1. Marinate the chicken ★★

- **Chicken**—Pat dry.
- **Brasa Mix**—Combine all the ingredients in a zip-top plastic bag and shake well.
- Place the chicken and 3 tablespoons of olive oil into the zip-top bag. Seal and move around the chicken to make sure it is well coated.
- Marinate in the refrigerator for at least 2 hours or up to overnight.

### 2. Prep the ingredients ★★

- Preheat the oven to 425°F.
- **Potatoes**—Scrub and cut in half if very big. Place the potatoes in a pot and cover with salted water.
- **Green beans**—Trim the ends.
- **Garlic**—Peel and mince.
- **Lime**—Cut in half and juice.
- **Aji Verde Mix**—Combine all the ingredients in a small bowl and mix well.

### 3. Roast the chicken ★★★

- Line a baking sheet with aluminum foil and lightly grease it with olive oil.
- Remove the chicken from the marinade and shake off the excess. Arrange the chicken skin-side up in single layer on the prepared baking sheet.
- Roast until the chicken is cooked through and registers an internal temperature of 165°F, 30 to 35 minutes.

### 4. Prep the potatoes (while the chicken is roasting) ★★★

- Set the pot of potatoes over medium-high heat and bring to a boil.
- Cook for 7 to 8 minutes. They will not be cooked through and that's okay.
- Drain the potatoes in a colander and return them to the pot.
- Add 2 tablespoons of olive oil, 1 teaspoon of salt, and pepper to taste and toss to combine.
- Spread out the potatoes evenly on a baking sheet and roast them in the oven for 20 minutes.
- Shake and turn the potatoes and continue roasting until the potatoes are deep brown and crispy all over, 5 to 6 more minutes.

### 5. Prep the Aji Verde sauce and green beans (while the chicken and potatoes are roasting) ★

- In a bowl, combine the mayonnaise, Aji Verde Mix, 2 teaspoons of lime juice, 1 tablespoon of olive oil, 2 tablespoons of Parmesan cheese, remaining ¼ teaspoon of salt, and pepper to taste. Mix well and set aside.
- In a large skillet, heat the remaining 1 tablespoon of olive oil over medium-high heat until hot.
- Add the garlic and a pinch of red pepper flakes (optional) and sauté for 1 minute. Add the green beans and 2 tablespoons water. Cover and cook until the beans are bright green and crisp-tender, 3 to 5 minutes.

### 6. Serve your dish ★

- Adjust the top oven rack to 6 inches below the broiler. Preheat the broiler to high.
- Broil the chicken until golden-brown and crispy, 2 to 3 minutes.
- Serve the chicken topped with the Aji Verde sauce and the roasted potatoes and sautéed green beans on the side.

# Mexico

As part of the two oldest civilizations, Aztec and Mayan, Mexico has local traditions of food and culture that date back 3,000 years. The basis of Mexican cuisine revolves around corn, beans, and chiles. Corn can be found in almost every meal, usually in the form of a tortilla! Did you know Mexican cuisine was one of the first culinary heritages to be added to the UNESCO's Intangible Cultural Heritage?

¡Buen provecho!
(bwen pro-BAY-cho)
*"Enjoy your meal!" in Spanish*

## YOU'LL COOK:

**Black Beans and Vegetables Wrapped in Corn Tortillas (Enchiladas)**

**Marinated Grilled Meat on Tortillas with Guacamole and Lime Crema (Fajitas)**

**Pork Tacos with Pineapple Salsa and Mexican Street Corn (Carnitas Tacos)**

## DID YOU KNOW...

- Mexico is located along the world's most violent earthquake zone called the Ring of Fire.

- Mexico City (the capital of Mexico) is sinking at a rate of 6 to 8 inches a year because it was built over an ancient lake bed and as the water has drained away, the ground has compacted beneath the city.

- The world's smallest dog breed, the Chihuahua, is the name of a Mexican state.

- Mexico has one of the Seven Wonders of the World—the Chichen Itza Pyramid, a Mayan ruin on Mexico's Yucatán Peninsula.

# Black Beans and Vegetables Wrapped in Corn Tortillas
## Enchiladas

Enchilada comes from the word "enchilar," meaning to season with chile. It's a traditional Mexican corn tortilla dish from Mayan times (1000 BCE–1697 CE). Corn tortillas are rolled around a meat and vegetable filling and then topped with a red chile sauce. In this recipe, we've opted to use flour tortillas and we've added chocolate to the sauce, which adds richness and depth to the dish.

 **SERVES**
4

 **ALLERGENS**
Nut-Free, Vegetarian

 **TOTAL PREP & COOK TIME**
45 minutes

## What You'll Need

1 small onion

1 red bell pepper

3 ounces (about ¼ head) broccoli

1 (15-oz) can black beans

Chopped fresh cilantro (optional)

1 tablespoon olive oil

6 ounces baby spinach

½ teaspoon salt

8 large flour tortillas

8 ounces shredded Monterey Jack cheese

1 cup sour cream (optional)

### E2E CHILI MIX

½ teaspoon ground cumin

½ teaspoon chili powder

½ teaspoon paprika

½ teaspoon granulated garlic

½ teaspoon ground cinnamon

¼ teaspoon sugar

### CHA-CHA! ENCHILADA SAUCE

4 tablespoons tomato sauce

2 tablespoons red chile sauce

1½ teaspoons oil

1½ teaspoons tomato paste

1 teaspoon chili powder

1 teaspoon granulated garlic

1 teaspoon ground cumin

1 teaspoon onion powder

1 teaspoon vegetable bouillon

1 teaspoon cocoa powder

½ teaspoon ground cinnamon

½ teaspoon sugar

½ teaspoon salt

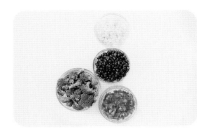

### 1. Prep the ingredients ★★

- Preheat the oven to 400°F.
- **Onion**—Peel and dice.
- **Bell pepper**—Cut in half, discard the stem and seeds, and dice.
- **Broccoli**—Trim the ends. Cut into small florets.
- **Black beans**—Drain and rinse in a colander.
- **Cilantro (optional)**—Cut off the stems and rinse well. Finely chop the leaves.
- **e2e Chili Mix**—Combine all the ingredients in a small bowl and mix well.

### 2. Sauté the vegetables ★★

- In a large skillet, heat 1 tablespoon of olive oil over medium heat until hot.
- Add the onion, bell pepper, and broccoli and sauté until tender, 3 to 5 minutes.
- Add the e2e Chili Mix, black beans, spinach, and ½ teaspoon of salt. Stir until the spinach has wilted.

### 3. Prep the enchilada sauce ★

- **Cha-cha! Enchilada Sauce**—Combine all the ingredients and 2 cups water in a medium bowl and mix well.

### 4. Assemble the enchiladas ★★

- Evenly coat the bottom of 9-by-13-inch baking dish with ¼ cup of Cha-cha! Enchilada Sauce.
- Place ¼ cup of the sautéed vegetables in the center of a tortilla.
- Roll it up tightly and place it in the baking dish, seam-side down.
- Repeat with the remaining tortillas and filling.
- Spread the remaining Cha-cha! Enchilada Sauce evenly over the enchiladas. Top with the Monterey Jack cheese.

### 5. Bake the enchiladas ★★★

- Place the baking dish on the middle rack in the oven and bake for 15 to 20 minutes, or until bubbly and golden brown.

### 6. Serve your dish ★★★

- Remove from the oven and let the enchiladas rest for 10 minutes.
- Using a spatula, place 2 enchiladas on each plate. Optional: Garnish with chopped cilantro and serve with dollops of sour cream.

# Marinated Grilled Meat on Tortillas with Guacamole and Lime Crema
## Fajitas

Fajitas (fah-HEE-tahs) are a classic Tex-Mex fusion dish that defies the borders dividing Mexico from the United States. Slices of grilled meat and vegetables are wrapped in soft flour tortillas and served with sour cream. In our version, we sauté the meat and vegetables in a skillet instead of grilling. We add some spices to the sour cream to create a spiced crema that complements the flavors of the fajitas.

**SERVES**
4

**ALLERGENS**
Nut-Free,
Gluten-Free Optional,
Vegetarian Optional

**TOTAL PREP & COOK TIME**
35 minutes

### What You'll Need

1 small red onion

1 bell pepper, any color

1 plum tomato

1 lime

2 avocados

10 sprigs cilantro

8 ounces queso fresco or Cheddar cheese

1½ pounds flank steak or boneless skinless chicken breast

1¾ teaspoons salt

½ teaspoon pepper, plus more as needed

1 tablespoon olive oil

½ cup sour cream

8 flour or corn tortillas

### Vegetarian Option

6 large portobello mushrooms

1 bell pepper, any color

### FIERY FAJITA SPICE MIX

2 teaspoons ground cumin

1¼ teaspoons dried oregano

1¼ teaspoons granulated garlic

1 teaspoon chili powder

½ teaspoon cayenne pepper

### 1. Prep the ingredients ★★

- **Red onion**—Peel and dice. Reserve 2 tablespoons for step 4 and use the rest in step 3.
- **Bell pepper**—Cut in half, discard the stem and seeds, and cut into ¼-inch slices.
- **Tomato**—Trim the ends and dice.
- **Lime**—Cut in half and juice. Use half in step 4 and half in step 5.
- **Avocados**—Cut in half lengthwise, then twist and separate the avocados halves. Using a spoon, remove the pits and scoop out the flesh.
- **Cilantro**—Cut off the stems and rinse well. Roughly chop the leaves.
- **Queso fresco or Cheddar cheese**—Crumble or shred.
- **Fiery Fajita Spice mix**—Combine all the ingredients in a small bowl and mix well.

### 2. Prep the steak or chicken ★★★

- Using a sharp knife, cut the steak or chicken against the grain into ¼-inch slices.

**Vegetarian option**

- **Portobello mushrooms**—Trim the stems and cut into ¼-inch slices.
- **Bell peppers**—Cut in half, discard the stem and seeds, and cut into ¼-inch slices.
- In a large bowl, combine the steak, chicken, or mushrooms, Fiery Fajita Spice Mix, 1 teaspoon of salt, and ½ teaspoon of pepper and toss well to coat.

### 3. Cook the fajitas ★★

- In a large skillet, heat 1 tablespoon of olive oil over medium heat until hot.
- Add the onion and bell peppers and sauté until tender, 3 to 5 minutes.
- Add the steak, chicken, or mushrooms and sauté until they are cooked through, about 5 minutes.
- If the pan looks dry, add water, 1 tablespoon at a time.

### 4. Make the guacamole ★

- In a bowl, combine the reserved red onion, avocado, diced tomato, cilantro, half the lime juice, ½ teaspoon of salt, and pepper to taste and mash with a fork.

### 5. Prep the lima crema and tortillas ★

- In a small bowl, whisk together the sour cream, remaining lime juice, remaining ¼ teaspoon of salt, and pepper to taste.
- Place the tortillas on a microwave-safe plate. Cover with a paper towel and heat for about 10 seconds until pliable.

### 6. Serve your dish ★

- Fill the warm tortillas with the meat or mushroom mixture. Top with dollops of the guacamole and lima crema.
- Sprinkle with the queso fresco or Cheddar cheese.

# Pork Tacos with Pineapple Salsa and Mexican Street Corn
## Carnitas Tacos

"Carnitas" means "little meats" in Spanish, and this dish heralds from the Mexican state of Michoacan. Boneless pork shoulder along with sweet citrusy oranges and a traditional spice mix is braised in the oven or slow-cooked until meltingly soft and tender. The meat is then shredded and served on warm corn tortillas and topped with a sweet pineapple salsa, the perfect tangy contrast to the flavorful and rich pork.

 **SERVES**
4

 **ALLERGENS**
Dairy-Free, Nut-Free, Gluten-Free, Vegetarian Optional

 **TOTAL PREP & COOK TIME**
2 hours 20 minutes + 2 hours or up to overnight to marinate

### What You'll Need

2½ pounds boneless pork shoulder or boneless, skinless chicken thighs

4 garlic cloves

2 oranges

1 red onion

2 limes

2 radishes

10 sprigs cilantro

1 (20-oz) can diced pineapple

1 tablespoon plus ¼ teaspoon salt

½ teaspoon olive oil

Pepper

4 ears corn

4 tablespoons butter

½ cup grated cotija cheese

Cayenne pepper (optional)

12 corn tortillas

### Vegetarian Option

2 (15-oz) cans chickpeas

2 pounds mixed mushrooms (white, cremini, shiitake, oyster)

### TACO TUESDAY MIX

2 teaspoons ground cumin

2 teaspoons granulated garlic

1½ teaspoons chili powder

1 teaspoon paprika

1 teaspoon dried oregano

### 1. Marinate the meat or vegetables ★★

- **Pork or chicken**—Trim the fat. Pork—Cut into large chunks. Chicken—Leave whole.
- **Garlic**—Peel and mince or crush with a garlic press.
- **Oranges**—Cut one orange in half and juice. Cut the other into quarters.
- **Taco Tuesday Mix**—Combine all the ingredients in a small bowl and mix well.

**Vegetarian option**

- **Chickpeas**—Drain and rinse.
- **Mushrooms**—Rinse and trim the ends. Cut into 1-inch pieces.

- In a large bowl, add the pork, chicken, or mushrooms and chickpeas, Taco Tuesday Mix, onion, garlic, orange juice, and orange quarters. Mix well.
- Cover and marinate in the refrigerator for at least 2 hours or overnight.

### 2. Prep the ingredients ★★

- Preheat the oven to 380°F.
- **Red onion**—Peel and dice. Save three-fourths for step 3 and one-fourth for step 4.
- **Limes**—Cut in half and juice 3 halves. Use 1 teaspoon for step 3 and the rest for step 4. Cut the remaining half into wedges for garnish.
- **Radishes**—Trim the ends and cut into thin coins.
- **Cilantro**—Cut off the stems and rinse well. Finely chop the leaves.
- **Diced pineapple**—Drain.

### 3. Cook the carnitas ★★

- In a Dutch oven or heavy-bottomed pot, combine the pork, chicken, or mushroom mixture, three-fourths of the diced onion, 1 teaspoon of lime juice, and 1 tablespoon of salt.
- Cover, place in the oven, and braise until very tender, about 2 hours for pork, 1 hour for chicken, or 30 minutes for the mushroom mixture.
- Meat option only—Shred the meat with two forks.
- Adjust the top oven rack to 6 inches below the broiler. Preheat the broiler to high.
- Transfer the shredded meat or mushroom mixture to a baking sheet and spread in an even layer. Broil until the meat or mushrooms are browned and slightly crisp, 4 to 5 minutes.

Continued...

# Pork Tacos with Pineapple Salsa and Mexican Street Corn
## Carnitas Tacos

4. **Assemble the pineapple salsa (while the meat or vegetables are in the oven)** ★

- In a large bowl, whisk together ½ teaspoon of olive oil, 1 teaspoon of lime juice, remaining ¼ teaspoon of salt, and pepper to taste.
- Add the pineapple, remaining red onion, radishes, and 3 tablespoons chopped cilantro.

5. **Prepare the Mexican corn and tortillas (30 minutes before the meat or vegetables are finished cooking)** ★ ★

- **Corn with husks**—Place the corn directly in the oven.
- **Corn without husks**—Wrap each ear of corn in aluminum foil and place them in the oven.
- Roast the corn until tender and cooked through, about 30 minutes.
- When the corn is cool enough to handle, remove the husks, if necessary, and rub each ear of corn with 1 tablespoon of butter. Sprinkle with the cotija cheese, cayenne pepper (optional), remaining cilantro, and a little lime juice.
- Warm up the tortillas by wrapping them in aluminum foil and placing them in the oven.

6. **Serve your dish** ★

- Arrange the carnitas on a platter along with the cooking juices and serve immediately with the warm tortillas, pineapple salsa, lime wedges, and Mexican corn on the side.

## DID YOU KNOW...

Mexico is the birthplace of chocolate. The ancient Mayans and Aztecs were the first to cultivate cacao beans and create a beverage known as xocoatl, which served as the precursor to modern chocolate.

# USA

If you think about it, nearly all the most popular American foods, like pizza, hamburgers, hot dogs, and apple pie, originally came from other countries. They were introduced to the United States over the years by colonists, settlers, and immigrants, starting in the early 1600s when European settlers began adapting their recipes by using the local American ingredients such as corn, beans, and squash.

## YOU'LL COOK:

**Maryland Crab Cakes with Coleslaw and Lemon Wedges**

**Spaghetti Squash "Pasta" with Bolognese Sauce**

**Eggplant Parmesan with Green Salad**

**Pulled Chicken BBQ on Rolls with Fresh Corn and Tomato Salad**

**Cajun Blackened Fish or Tofu with Succotash and Rice**

**Southern Beef or Vegetable Chili with Corn Muffins**

- One of the most iconic symbols of the United States, the Statue of Liberty, was a gift from the people of France to the United States in 1886.

- The United States has the longest cave system in the world! Mammoth Cave National Park is a limestone labyrinth of 426 miles mapped and explored. The park estimates a potential for another 600 miles in its system yet to be explored!

- Morocco was the first country to formally recognize the United States as an independent nation in 1786 with a treaty of friendship and peace.

# Maryland Crab Cakes
## with Coleslaw and Lemon Wedges

No dish exemplifies the mid-Atlantic coastline and, specifically, the state of Maryland, more than the crab cake. It was one of the first Native American dishes adopted by the settlers of the Chesapeake Bay region probably because crab was so plentiful in its waters.

 **SERVES**
4

 **ALLERGENS**
Dairy-Free, Nut-Free, Vegetarian Optional

 **TOTAL PREP & COOK TIME**
35 minutes

## What You'll Need

1 lemon

1 medium red onion

1 red bell pepper

½ small head green cabbage

1 large carrot

2 tablespoons olive oil

½ teaspoon salt, plus more as needed

1 pound super lump crabmeat

2 large eggs (for crabmeat option only)

¼ cup mayonnaise

¼ teaspoon sugar

Pepper

## Vegetarian Option

2 (14-oz) cans hearts of palm

½ cup mayonnaise

## CRABBY BAY MIX

1 cup panko or breadcrumbs

1½ tablespoons Old Bay Seasoning

## KOOLSLA HERBIE MIX

1 teaspoon lemon peel granules

1 teaspoon celery seed

1 teaspoon dried parsley

### 1. Prep the ingredients ★★

- **Lemon**—Cut in half. Juice one half for step 4. Cut the second half into wedges for step 6.
- **Red onion**—Cut in half. Dice one half for step 2. Thinly slice the second half for step 4.
- **Bell pepper**—Cut in half, discard the stem and seeds, and dice.
- **Cabbage**—Thinly slice using a large knife.
- **Carrot**—Peel, trim the ends, and shred using a grater.
- **Crabby Bay Mix**—Combine all the ingredients in a small bowl and mix well.
- **Koolsla Herbie Mix**—Combine all the ingredients in a small bowl and mix well.

**Vegetarian option**
- **Hearts of palm**—Drain and finely chop into small chunks.

### 2. Sauté the vegetables ★★

- In a large skillet, heat 1 tablespoon of olive oil over medium-high heat until hot.
- Add the diced red onion, bell pepper, and a pinch of salt and sauté until tender, 3 to 5 minutes.
- Remove from the heat and let cool.

### 3. Form the crab cakes ★

- In a large bowl, gently combine the Crabby Bay Mix, sautéed vegetables, crabmeat, and eggs.

**Vegetarian option**
- In a large bowl, combine the Crabby Bay Mix, sautéed vegetables, hearts of palm, and vegan mayonnaise.
- Using your hands, form the crab or hearts of palm mixture into eight 3-inch patties.
- Place the crab cakes on a baking sheet, refrigerate until firm, at least 10 minutes.

### 4. Make the coleslaw ★

- In a large bowl, whisk together the Koolsla Herbie Mix, 1 teaspoon of lemon juice, ¼ cup of mayonnaise, ¼ teaspoon of sugar, ½ teaspoon of salt, and pepper to taste.
- Add the cabbage, carrot, and sliced red onion and toss until fully coated with the dressing.

### 5. Cook the crab cakes ★★

- In a large nonstick or cast-iron skillet, heat the remaining 1 tablespoon of olive oil over medium-high heat until hot.
- Working in batches, cook 3 or 4 crab cakes, being careful not to overcrowd the skillet.
- Cook until golden brown and cooked through, 2 to 3 minutes per side.

### 6. Serve your dish ★

- Place 2 crab cakes and a lemon wedge on each plate. Serve with the coleslaw on the side.

# Spaghetti Squash "Pasta"
## with Bolognese Sauce

Spaghetti squash is a winter varietal with a slightly stringy flesh that originally came from China, though the seeds arrived in the United States in the 1930s. It has become a popular vegetable to grow and eat. With a texture and appearance of spaghetti, it works well topped with this delicious meat sauce, making this dish gluten-free. Bolognese sauce originated in Italy, but it has become a huge hit in the States, particularly in regions with a large number of Italian immigrants.

 **SERVES**
4

 **ALLERGENS**
Nut-Free, Gluten-Free, Vegetarian Optional

 **TOTAL PREP & COOK TIME**
1 hour 20 minutes

## What You'll Need

3 tablespoons olive oil, plus more as needed

2 spaghetti squash (see note in step 1)

2½ teaspoons salt

Pepper

1 onion

1 carrot

1 celery stalk

2 sprigs fresh basil (optional)

1½ pounds ground beef

8 ounces ground pork

2 (15-oz) cans crushed tomatoes

1 cup whole milk

½ teaspoon sugar

3 ounces grated Pecorino Romano cheese

## Vegetarian Option

8 ounces cremini mushrooms

1 (8-oz) package tempeh

## Herbie Herb Mix

2 teaspoons dried oregano

2 teaspoons dried basil

2 teaspoons dried thyme

2 teaspoons granulated garlic

¼ teaspoon red pepper flakes

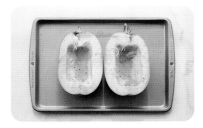

1. **Roast the spaghetti squash** ★★★

- Preheat the oven to 375°F. Lightly grease a baking sheet with olive oil.
- **Spaghetti squash**—Cut in half lengthwise. Using a spoon, scoop out the seeds and stringy bits of flesh and discard.
- Rub 1 tablespoon of olive oil over the squash halves. Sprinkle with 1 teaspoon of salt and pepper to taste.
- Place both halves, cut-side down, on the prepared baking sheet.
- Roast until the flesh has softened, 20 to 25 minutes. Remove from the oven and let cool.
- Note: If spaghetti squash is not available, serve with spaghetti pasta. Cook the pasta in salted boiling water until al dente, 8 to 10 minutes. Drain the pasta in a colander.

2. **Prep the ingredients (while baking the squash)** ★★

- **Onion**—Peel and dice.
- **Carrot**—Peel and dice.
- **Celery**—Trim the ends and dice.
- **Basil (optional)**—Remove the leaves and rinse. Stack the leaves and thinly slice.
- **Herbie Herb Mix**—Combine all the ingredients in a small bowl and mix well.

**Vegetarian option**

- **Mushrooms**—Rinse and finely chop.
- **Tempeh**—Crumble into small pieces.

3. **Prepare the Bolognese sauce** ★★

- In a Dutch oven or deep skillet, heat 1 tablespoon of olive oil over medium-high heat until hot.
- Add the onion and sauté until soft, 1 to 2 minutes.
- Add the ground beef and pork or the mushrooms and tempeh and cook, using a fork to crumble the meat or tempeh, until browned through, 5 to 7 minutes.
- Add the carrot, celery, and Herbie Herb Mix and cook until the vegetables are almost tender, about 5 minutes.
- Add the crushed tomatoes, 1 cup of milk, remaining 1½ teaspoons of salt, ½ teaspoon of sugar, and pepper to taste and stir to combine.
- Decrease the heat to medium-low and simmer until the sauce has thickened, about 20 minutes.

4. **Prepare the spaghetti squash noodles** ★

- Once the roasted squash is cool enough to handle, use a fork to gently scrape out the flesh into spaghetti-like strings.
- Place the "noodles" in a large bowl and drizzle with the remaining 1 tablespoon of olive oil. Toss to coat.

5. **Serve your dish** ★

- Divide the spaghetti squash "noodles" among individual bowls and top with the Bolognese sauce. Garnish with the grated Pecorino Romano cheese and fresh basil (optional).

# Eggplant Parmesan
## with Green Salad

Alla Parmigiana ("with Parmesan") is a typical American-Italian dish made by dredging and frying veal, chicken, or eggplant in a mixture of breadcrumbs and Parmesan cheese. Enjoy it alongside a green salad with balsamic and shallot vinaigrette. Kids will learn how to dredge eggplant slices, which is the perfect task for any age.

**SERVES**
4

**ALLERGENS**
Nut-Free, Vegetarian

**TOTAL PREP & COOK TIME**
1 hour 20 minutes

## What You'll Need

3 tablespoons olive oil, plus more as needed

2 medium eggplants

1¾ teaspoons salt, plus more as needed

½ cup cherry or grape tomatoes

1 head butter lettuce

1 shallot (optional)

2 large eggs

¼ cup all-purpose flour

1 cup panko or breadcrumbs

1 cup grated Parmesan cheese

Pepper

1 (28-oz) can tomato puree

½ teaspoon sugar

2 cups grated mozzarella cheese

1 tablespoon balsamic vinegar

½ teaspoon honey

## HERBIE HERB MIX

2 teaspoons dried oregano

2 teaspoons dried basil

2 teaspoons dried thyme

2 teaspoons granulated garlic

¼ teaspoon red pepper flakes

### 1. Prep the ingredients

- Preheat the oven to 400°F. Lightly grease 2 baking sheets with olive oil.
- **Eggplant**—Trim the ends and cut into ½-inch slices. Place the slices in a colander and generously sprinkle both sides of the slices with salt. Let sit over a bowl for 15 minutes until you see beads of water coming out of the eggplant. Rinse well with water and pat dry.
- **Cherry tomatoes**—Cut in half.
- **Lettuce**—Rinse thoroughly and roughly chop.
- **Shallot (optional)**—Peel and dice.
- **Herbie Herb Mix**—Combine all the ingredients in a small bowl and mix well.

### 2. Prep the eggplant ★

- Set up 2 bowls. Bowl 1: Whisk together the eggs with 1 tablespoon water. Bowl 2: Mix together ¼ cup of flour, 1 cup of panko or breadcrumbs, ½ cup of Parmesan cheese, ¼ teaspoon of salt, and pepper to taste.
- Using tongs, dip the eggplant slices into the egg mixture, covering both sides, and then do the same with the panko mixture. Use your hands to evenly coat both sides with panko.
- Place the slices on the prepared baking sheets and drizzle generously with olive oil.
- Bake until the eggplant is golden brown and tender, about 20 minutes total (flip halfway and drizzle with olive oil).

### 3. Make the marinara sauce ★★

- In a Dutch oven or large pot, heat 1 tablespoon of olive oil over medium-high heat.
- Add the tomato puree, Herbie Herb Mix, ½ teaspoon of salt, ½ teaspoon of sugar, and pepper to taste and stir well.
- Bring to a boil and let simmer for 10 minutes.

Continued...

# Eggplant Parmesan
## with Green Salad

### 4. Bake the eggplant Parmesan  ★★★

- In a bowl, combine the mozzarella cheese and the remaining ½ cup of Parmesan cheese. Spread out 1 cup of the marinara sauce on the bottom of the baking dish. Arrange half of the baked eggplant slices on top, overlapping if necessary.
- Spread 1 cup of the marinara sauce over the eggplant and sprinkle with ¾ cup of the cheese mixture. Repeat with the remaining eggplant and cheese mixture.
- Cover with aluminum foil and bake for 20 minutes.
- Remove the foil and bake for another 5 to 10 minutes, until the cheese is browned.

### 5. Make the salad  ★

- In a large bowl, whisk together the balsamic vinegar, remaining 2 tablespoons of olive oil, honey (optional), minced shallot (optional), remaining 1 teaspoon of salt, and pepper to taste.
- Add the lettuce and cherry tomatoes and toss to coat.

### 6. Serve your dish  ★

- Place a large serving of eggplant Parmesan on each plate and serve with a side of green salad.

## DID YOU KNOW...

United States has the most
national parks of any country
in the world. The National
Park Service manages over
400 parks, preserves, and
historic sites across the country,
including famous landmarks like
Yellowstone National Park and the
Grand Canyon.

# Pulled Chicken BBQ
## on Rolls with Fresh Corn and Tomato Salad

Backyard barbecues are virtually synonymous with American summers. The pulled chicken barbecue sandwiches are easy to assemble and fun to eat with friends and family; serve them with chilled lemonade while enjoying the sun on your backyard patio.

 **SERVES**
4

 **ALLERGENS**
Dairy-Free, Nut-Free, Gluten-Free Optional, Vegetarian Optional

 **TOTAL PREP & COOK TIME**
1 hour 10 minutes

### What You'll Need

1 medium onion

3 ears fresh corn or 2 (15-oz) cans corn kernels

8 ounces cherry tomatoes

4 scallions

½ lime

2 tablespoons olive oil

1½ pounds boneless skinless chicken thighs

1½ teaspoons salt

Pepper

4 potato rolls or gluten-free sandwich rolls

### Vegetarian Option

3 (15-oz) cans green jackfruit or 6 portobello mushrooms

### CIDERIN' BBQ SAUCE

1 cup ketchup

3 tablespoons apple cider

3 tablespoons brown sugar

2 tablespoons honey

1 tablespoon Worcestershire sauce

1 teaspoon onion powder

1 teaspoon granulated garlic

1 teaspoon salt

### 1. Prep the ingredients ★★

- Preheat the oven to 380°F.
- **Onion**—Peel and dice.
- **Fresh corn**—Shuck the corn. Lay an ear of corn flat on a cutting board and cut down the sides to remove the corn kernels. Rotate the cob and continue cutting and rotating until all the kernels are removed. Discard the corncob. OR **Canned corn**—Drain and rinse.
- **Cherry tomatoes**—Cut in half.
- **Scallions**—Trim the ends and cut into ⅛-inch slices.
- **Lime**—Juice.
- **Ciderin' BBQ Sauce**—Combine all the ingredients in a small bowl and mix well.

**Vegetarian option**

- **Green jackfruit**—Drain and cut into big chunks. OR **Portobello mushrooms**—Trim off the stems and cut into ¼-inch slices.

### 2. Prep the BBQ ★★★

- In a Dutch oven or heavy ovenproof pot with a lid, heat 1 tablespoon of olive oil over medium-high heat until hot.
- Add the onion and sauté until tender, about 2 minutes.
- Add the chicken or jackfruit or mushrooms, Ciderin' BBQ Sauce, ¼ cup water, and 1 teaspoon of salt and stir well.
- Bring to a simmer and cover with a lid.
- Place the covered pot in the oven and bake until the chicken or jackfruit or mushrooms is very tender, 40 to 45 minutes for chicken or 20 to 25 minutes for jackfruit or mushrooms.

### 3. Prep the salad (while the BBQ is in the oven) ★

- In a large serving bowl, whisk together 1 tablespoon of lime juice, remaining 1 tablespoon of olive oil, remaining ½ teaspoon of salt, and pepper to taste.
- Add the corn kernels, tomatoes, and scallions and stir to coat well.
- Cover the bowl with plastic wrap and refrigerate until ready to serve.

### 4. Assemble the pulled BBQ ★★

- Remove the pot from the oven.
- Use 2 forks to shred the chicken or jackfruit or mushrooms finely.
- If there is too much liquid, place the uncovered pot on the stove and cook over medium-high heat until the sauce achieves the desired thickness.

### 5. Serve the dish ★

- Lightly toast the sandwich rolls. Top with the pulled chicken or jackfruit or mushrooms. Serve with a side of the corn and tomato salad.

# Cajun Blackened Fish or Tofu
## with Succotash and Rice

Blackening is a traditional Cajun cooking technique. Fish is coated in a spice rub and cooked in a screaming-hot cast-iron skillet, which chars the spices. Typically, the rub is a blend of paprika, thyme, garlic powder, and cayenne pepper. Use a firm white fish like sea bass.

 **SERVES**
4

 **ALLERGENS**
Nut-Free, Gluten-Free, Vegetarian Optional

 **TOTAL PREP & COOK TIME**
25 minutes

### What You'll Need

1 lemon

1 small onion

6 ounces green beans

1 cup cherry tomatoes

1 (15-oz) can corn kernels

1 (15-oz) can lima beans

4 (6-oz) fish fillets

1½ cups basmati or other long-grain rice

½ teaspoon salt, plus more as needed

2 tablespoons olive oil

Pepper

### Vegetarian Option

2 (16-oz) packages firm tofu

### BLACKENIN' RUB

1 tablespoon sweet paprika

1 teaspoon celery seed

1 teaspoon salt

Pepper

¼ teaspoon lemon peel granules

### TARRA HERBIE MIX

2 teaspoons garlic powder

1½ teaspoons dried tarragon

1 teaspoon chicken or vegetable bouillon

½ teaspoon lemon peel granules

### 1. Prep the ingredients ★★

- **Lemon**—Cut into wedges.
- **Onion**—Peel and dice.
- **Green beans**—Trim the ends and cut into ½-inch pieces.
- **Cherry tomatoes**—Cut in half.
- **Corn**—Drain and rinse.
- **Lima beans**—Drain and rinse.
- **Tarra Herbie Mix**—Combine all the ingredients in a small bowl and mix well.
- **Blackenin' Rub**—Combine all the ingredients in a small bowl and mix well.
- **Fish**—Coat the fish evenly with the rub, cover, and let rest in the refrigerator for 15 minutes.

### Vegetarian option

- Tofu—Drain. Use paper towels to press out the liquid from the tofu. Cut into 1-inch cubes.
- Coat the tofu with Blackenin' Rub, cover, and let rest in the refrigerator for 15 minutes.

### 2. Cook the rice ★★

- Rinse the rice in a colander to remove excess starch.
- In a small pot, combine the rice, a pinch of salt, and 2¼ cups water. Bring to a boil over medium-high heat.
- Lower the heat, cover, and simmer until the liquid has been absorbed and the rice is tender, about 15 minutes.
- Remove from the heat, fluff the cooked rice with a fork, and keep warm until ready to serve.

### 3. Prep the succotash ★★

- In a large skillet, heat 1 tablespoon of olive oil over medium-high heat until hot.
- Add the onion and green beans and sauté until tender, 4 to 5 minutes.
- Add the corn kernels, lima beans, cherry tomatoes, Tarra Herbie Mix, ½ teaspoon of salt, and pepper to taste. Sauté for another 3 to 4 minutes. Keep warm while preparing the fish.

### 4. Prep the fish or tofu ★★

- In a nonstick skillet, heat the remaining 1 tablespoon of olive oil over medium-high heat until hot.
- Gently add the fish or tofu in one layer, being careful not to crowd the pan (cook in batches, if necessary).
- Cook until the fish or tofu begins to blacken, 3 to 4 minutes. Using a spatula, carefully flip the fish or tofu and cook for another 2 to 3 minutes.

### 5. Serve your dish ★

- Serve the blackened fish or tofu on individual plates with the rice, succotash, and lemon wedges alongside.

# Southern Beef or Vegetable Chili
## with Corn Muffins

Chili is a wholly American dish, though it takes advantage of typical Mexican spices. The earliest description of chili is from San Antonio, Texas, back in 1828, when they created it as a way to make a little meat go a long way by adding lots of beans. It was featured at the 1893 World Fair in Chicago, and by the Roaring '20s there were chili joints across the country.

**SERVES**
4

**ALLERGENS**
Nut-Free,
Gluten-Free Optional,
Vegetarian Optional

**TOTAL PREP & COOK TIME**
45 minutes

### What You'll Need

1 medium red onion

1 green bell pepper

1 (15-oz) can black beans

1 (15-oz) can red kidney beans

3 scallions (optional)

1 tablespoon olive oil

1 pound ground beef

1 (14-oz) can diced tomatoes

½ cup quinoa (optional)

1¾ teaspoons salt

Pepper

½ cup or 8 tablespoons butter, plus more as needed

1½ cups all-purpose flour or gluten-free flour

½ cup cornmeal

1 tablespoon baking powder

¼ cup sugar

½ cup milk

1 cup sour cream

1 large egg

6 ounces grated Monterey Jack cheese

### Vegetarian Option

2 medium sweet potatoes

### CHILIN' MIX

2 teaspoons ground cumin

2 teaspoons vegetable bouillon

1½ teaspoons chili powder

1½ teaspoons paprika

1½ teaspoons granulated garlic

1½ teaspoons dried oregano

1 teaspoon ground coriander

### 1. Prep the ingredients ★★

- Preheat the oven to 350°F.
- **Red onion**—Peel and dice.
- **Bell pepper**—Cut in half, discard the stem and seeds, and dice.
- **Black beans**—Drain and rinse.
- **Red kidney beans**—Drain and rinse.
- **Scallions (optional)**—Trim the ends and thinly slice.
- **Chilin' Mix**—Combine all the ingredients in a small bowl and mix well.

**Vegetarian option**

- **Sweet potatoes**—Peel and cut into ½-inch pieces.

### 2. Prep the chili ★★

- In a medium pot, heat 1 tablespoon of olive oil over medium-high heat until hot.
- Add the ground beef or sweet potatoes, onion, bell pepper, and Chilin' Mix and sauté, using a fork to crumble the ground beef, until the beef is browned or the potatoes are tender, about 5 minutes.
- Add the diced tomatoes, black beans, red kidney beans, ½ cup of quinoa (optional), 2 cups water, 1½ teaspoons of salt, and pepper to taste.
- Bring to a boil, then lower the heat to a simmer. Partially cover and simmer for 15 minutes. Add water as necessary if the chili gets too thick.
- Optional: To thicken the chili, roughly mash the beans with a fork.

### 3. Make the muffin batter (while the chili is cooking) ★★

- In a small microwave-safe bowl, melt 8 tablespoons of butter in the microwave for 30 to 40 seconds.
- In a medium bowl, combine 1½ cups of flour or gluten-free flour, ½ cup of cornmeal, 1 tablespoon of baking powder, ¼ cup of sugar, remaining ¼ teaspoon of salt, ½ cup of milk, ½ cup of sour cream, and melted butter.
- Whisk well to mix. Add the egg and whisk together until combined.

### 4. Bake the corn muffins (while the chili is cooking) ★

- Grease a 6-cup muffin pan with butter.
- Spoon the batter into the muffin cups.
- Place the muffin pan in the middle oven rack and bake until golden brown, 20 to 25 minutes. Insert a toothpick in the middle of a muffin and if it comes out clean, they are ready!

### 5. Serve your dish ★

- Ladle chili into soup bowls and top with dollops of the remaining ½ cup of sour cream, grated Monterey Jack cheese, and scallions (optional). Serve with the corn muffins.

# Glossary

**al dente**—It is translated from Italian into "firm to the bite." It's used to describe how long to cook pasta. Al dente is the preferred texture of cooked pasta—not too hard and not too soft.

**aonori**—It is an edible green powder made from dried seaweed, commonly used as a condiment or seasoning in Japanese cuisine.

**arugula**—Known also as rocket salad and rucola, it is a lettuce with a slightly peppery taste and is in the same family as broccoli, kale, and Brussels sprouts. A very healthy green!

**balsamic vinegar**—Originating from Italy, this vinegar is from grape must, which is freshly crushed grape juice that includes the skins, seeds, and stems of the fruit. It is often aged for many years, which gives it a sweeter flavor.

**berbere spice**—A key ingredient in Ethiopian and Eritrean cuisine, it is a spice blend combining dried chile peppers, paprika, ginger, garlic, fenugreek, coriander, cumin, cinnamon, cardamom, cloves, black pepper, allspice, and nutmeg.

**black rice vinegar**—Also known as Chinkiang vinegar or Zhenjiang vinegar, this vinegar originated in China and is made from fermented black glutinous rice.

**bok choy**—It is a type of leafy vegetable that is commonly used in Chinese cuisine. It belongs to the Brassica family, which also includes cabbage, kale, and broccoli.

**bonito flakes (katsuabushi)**—It is made from dried and smoked skipjack tuna, the smallest and most abundant type of tuna; skipjack tuna is also known as ocean bonitos.

**bouillon (chicken, beef, or vegetable)**—It is a flavorful concentrated liquid made from simmering meat, vegetables, and/or herbs in water, and is used as a base for soups, sauces, gravies, and other dishes.

**braising**—This is a cooking method in which an ingredient, usually meat, is browned over high heat and then simmered in liquid in a covered pot over lower heat.

**breading**—Breadcrumbs or crushed crackers are pressed into meats and then usually fried to create a flavorful crispy coating.

**broiling**—This method is used to quickly cook foods using high direct heat, with the goal to create a browned or crisp exterior without overcooking the interior.

**cannellini beans**—These are a white kidney-type bean, popular in the Mediterranean and particularly in Tuscany, Italy. These beans have a creamy texture and nutty flavor and can be used in salads, soups, and purees. Cannellini beans are fat-free and an excellent source of fiber, folate, iron, and magnesium.

**cassava flour**—It is a type of flour made from the cassava root, which is a starchy tuberous root vegetable native to South America.

**celery root**—It is also known as celeriac. It is a root vegetable that is part of the celery family. Celery root has a distinct flavor that is similar to celery stalks, but with a slightly nutty and earthy undertone.

**chickpeas**—These are also known as garbanzo beans. It is a type of legume that provides a good source of protein, fiber, and various vitamins and minerals.

**chorizo**—It is a type of sausage that originated in Spain and is commonly used in Spanish, Mexican, and Portuguese cuisines. It is made from ground meat (usually pork), seasoned with various spices, and typically cured or smoked to develop its distinct flavor.

**coconut milk**—This is the milky liquid extracted from grated coconut flesh and it has a high fat content. It generally comes in cans. The coconut milk in cartons found in the refrigerated section of the grocery store is more watery and thin.

**cotija cheese**—It is a type of hard, crumbly cheese made from cow's milk that originated in Mexico. It is named after the town of Cotija in the state of Michoacán.

**couscous**—It is a type of small pasta made from durum wheat semolina. It is a staple food in many North African countries, particularly in Morocco, where it is traditionally served as a base for stews and other dishes.

**crème fraîche**—It is a thick, cultured cream that originated in France. It is made by fermenting cream with lactic acid bacteria, which thickens the cream and gives it a distinctive tangy taste.

**curry powder**—It is a blend of many different spices, seeds, and herbs. The most common ingredients in curry powder include cardamom, cinnamon, coriander, cumin, tamarind, and turmeric. The bright color of turmeric is what gives curry powder its characteristic vibrant yellow color.

**deglaze**—It is a cooking method that involves using liquid, typically wine or broth, to dissolve the browned bits of food that stick to the bottom of a pan after searing, sautéing, or roasting.

**doubanjiang/spicy fermented bean paste**—It is a popular Chinese condiment made from fermented broad beans, soybeans, salt, rice, and various spices. It originated in the Sichuan province of China and is used in many Sichuan dishes.

**emulsify**—It refers to the process of combining two or more liquids that usually do not mix together, such as oil and water, into a stable mixture by using an emulsifying agent. Common emulsifying agents used in cooking include egg yolks, mustard, honey, mayonnaise, vinegar, and lecithin (found in egg yolks and soybeans).

**escarole**—This is a member of the chicory family and sometimes called broad-leaved endive. It has a mildly bitter taste and can be used in salads or chopped and added to warm soups.

**farro**—It is a type of ancient wheat grain that has been used for thousands of years as a staple food in Mediterranean and Middle Eastern cuisines. It has a nutty flavor and chewy texture and is rich in fiber, protein, and other nutrients.

**fenugreek**—It is a spice that is commonly used in Indian, Middle Eastern, and North African cuisines. Fenugreek seeds are small and yellowish-brown and have a distinctive aroma and slightly bitter taste.

**fish sauce**—It is a condiment made from fermented fish, usually anchovies or other small fish, that is widely used in Southeast Asian cuisines, particularly in Thai, Vietnamese, and Filipino cooking. It is typically made by fermenting fish in salt for an extended period of time, often several months to a year or more.

**folding**—This is a technique of gently mixing delicate ingredients, usually using a rubber or silicone spatula.

**garam masala**—It is a spice blend commonly used in Indian, Pakistani, and South Asian cuisines. The word "garam" refers to the Ayurvedic phrase for "heating the body," as it was believed the spice could be used medicinally to elevate body temperature. It is made by roasting the spices and grinding them into a powder, consisting of black and white peppercorns, cloves, cinnamon, nutmeg, black and green cardamom pods, bay leaf, cumin seeds, and coriander.

**gochujang paste**—It is a Korean fermented chile paste that is made from red chile pepper powder, glutinous rice powder, fermented soybean powder, salt, and sometimes other ingredients like sweeteners and/or garlic. The mixture is fermented for several months to develop its distinct flavor profile.

**hearts of palm**—These come from the core of certain palm trees and are often used as an alternative to animal proteins by vegetarians.

**jackfruit**—It is a large tropical fruit that is native to South and Southeast Asia. It is the largest tree-borne fruit and can weigh up to 80 pounds when fully grown.

**kizami beni shoga**—It is a type of Japanese pickled ginger that is thinly sliced. It is made from fresh ginger root that is pickled in a mixture of vinegar, sugar, and salt.

**lemongrass**—It is a tropical herb that is widely used in Southeast Asian cuisine. It is known for its distinct citrusy flavor and aroma, resembling a combination of lemon and herbaceous notes. Lemongrass is used in various forms, including fresh, dried, and powdered, and is a popular ingredient in soups, curries, marinades, teas, and other dishes.

**lentils**—They are small, lens-shaped legumes that are commonly used in cooking and known for their high nutritional value (rich source of protein, fiber, and various essential nutrients). They come in various colors, including green, brown, red, and yellow.

**marinating**—the soaking of meats, seafood, and sometimes vegetables in a savory liquid—sometimes for long periods of time—to improve flavor or to tenderize the ingredient.

**mirin**—It is a sweet rice wine that is commonly used in Japanese cuisine as a seasoning ingredient. It is made from fermented rice and has a sweet, syrupy consistency with a slightly tangy flavor.

**mung beans**—They are small green legumes and are highly nutritious. They are a good source of plant-based protein, dietary fiber, vitamins, and minerals.

**naan**—It is a type of flatbread that is popular in many South Asian and Middle Eastern cuisines. It is typically made from wheat flour, water, salt, and yeast and is traditionally cooked in a tandoor, which is a clay oven.

**nori**—It is a type of edible seaweed, typically used in sushi. Nori is made from several species of red algae that are harvested, washed, and then dried into thin sheets.

**nutritional yeast**—It is a type of deactivated yeast that is often used as a condiment in vegetarian and vegan cooking. It is typically grown on molasses or sugar cane, then harvested, washed, and dried to create a flaky or powdery texture. Nutritional yeast has a savory, slightly cheesy flavor and is often used to add umami depth to dishes.

**okonomiyaki**—This is a savory Japanese pancake made with a batter of flour, eggs, grated vegetables, and often meat or seafood, cooked on a griddle or pan, and typically topped with a variety of condiments and sauces.

**orzo**—A small oval-shaped pasta that looks a little bit like rice.

**oyster sauce**—It is traditionally used in Cantonese cooking. It is a thick brown sauce made from cooked oysters, sugar, salt, and water, and thickened with cornstarch.

**panko**—It is a type of Japanese breadcrumb that is known for its light and crispy texture. It is made from white bread without crusts, which is processed into flakes, and then baked or toasted to create a crispy texture.

**paprika**—It is a spice made from dried and ground red peppers. It is known for its vibrant red color and distinct flavor, which can range from mild and sweet to hot and pungent, depending on the type of paprika and the peppers used.

**pickling**—A method of preserving foods by storing them immersed in an acidic liquid.

**pine nuts**—They are the edible seeds of pine trees. They are small, elongated seeds with a delicate flavor and creamy texture, and are a popular ingredient in Mediterranean, Middle Eastern, and Italian cuisines.

**puff pastry**—It is a flaky and buttery pastry dough that is used to make a variety of sweet and savory baked goods. It is made by repeatedly folding and rolling layers of dough and butter to create a laminated dough with distinct layers that puff up when baked, resulting in a light and airy texture.

**queso fresco**—It means "fresh cheese" in Spanish. It is a crumbly and mild cheese that is commonly used in Latin American cuisine. It is light and mild and a perfect accompaniment to either heavy or light dishes. It doesn't melt, it crumbles.

**quinoa**—It is not a grain! They are seeds from the quinoa plant, which is in the same family as Swiss chard and spinach. It was originally grown in the Andes region of South America as one of the few crops the ancient Incas could grow at such high altitudes. It is an excellent source of protein.

**roasting**—Foods are cooked using dry heat that surrounds it in the oven.

**saffron**—It is the world's most expensive spice by weight. Saffron is the bright red stigmas of crocus flowers, which flower once a year in the fall in countries like Greece, India, Iran, Afghanistan, and Spain.

**sake**—Japanese wine made from fermented rice.

**sautéing**—It is a cooking method that uses a small amount of oil or fat and cooks an ingredient over high heat, usually with continuous or frequent stirring.

**scallions**—They are also known as green onions or spring onions. They are a type of young onion with a mild flavor that is commonly used in cooking for their fresh and oniony taste.

**simmering**—Foods are cooked in hot liquids that are kept just below the boiling point.

**skewers**—Thin metal or wood sticks that are used to thread chunks of food onto and then cooked.

**stewing**—It is a cooking method that involves cooking food slowly in a liquid, typically with low heat, for an extended period of time.

**stir-frying**—Cooking meat or vegetables over high heat while constantly stirring it to avoid burning.

**sumac**—It comes from the deep red berries of a wild Mediterranean bush, found in southern Italy and parts of the Middle East. It is an essential ingredient in Arabic cooking, being preferred to lemon for sourness and astringency.

**Swiss chard**—It is a leafy green vegetable that is a member of the beet family. It is known for its large, dark green leaves and colorful stems that come in various shades of red, yellow, orange, pink, and white.

**tahini**—It is a paste made from ground sesame seeds that is commonly used in Middle Eastern, Mediterranean, and North African cuisines. It has a rich and nutty flavor and a creamy texture.

**tapas**—They are a style of Spanish cuisine that consists of small, flavorful dishes that are typically served as appetizers or snacks.

**teff flour**—It is a type of flour made from the grain of teff, which is a tiny, gluten-free grain native to Ethiopia and Eritrea. It is used to make a variety of traditional foods, including injera (a type of Ethiopian sourdough flatbread) and porridges.

**tempeh**—A plant-based food made with fermented soybeans. It is pressed together, cut into slices or crumbled, and cooked.

**tofu**—It is made by coagulating soy milk and then molding the curds into brick shapes, similar to the way cheese is made out of milk. It provides a healthy source of protein for vegetarian or vegan diets. Tofu comes in various forms including silken, firm, extra-firm, puffed, smoked, and fermented.

**to taste**—It is commonly used in cooking and culinary instructions, and it refers to the amount of an ingredient that should be added to a dish based on personal preference.

**tomato paste**—It is a thick, concentrated tomato product made from cooking down tomatoes to reduce their moisture content.

**turmeric**—It is a bright yellow spice that comes from the root of the *Curcuma longa* plant, which is native to South Asia. It has anti-inflammatory properties.

# Index